<u>40 Top Marketing</u> <u>Mistakes</u>

<u>Towards More Effective Video Marketing</u>

Dennis E. Bradford, Ph.D.

Books by the Same Author

The Fundamental Ideas

The Three Things the Rest of Us Should Know about Zen Training

The Meditative Approach to Philosophy

How to Survive College Emotionally

Mastery in 7 Steps

Emotional Eating

Personal Transformation

How to Eat Less – Easily!

Compulsive Overeating Help

Getting Things Done

How to Stop Emotional Eating

How to Become Happily Published

With Anna Wright: *Belly Fat Blast*

Weight Lifting

Love and Respect

12 Publicity Mistakes that Keep Marketers Poor

It's Not Just About the Money!

Acknowledgements

I thank all those who taught me about marketing and videos including Dan Ardebili, Peter Beattie, Lou D'Alo, Keith Dougherty, Jim Edwards, Ken Evoy, Jason Fladlien, Seth Godin, Ross Goldberg, Todd Gross, Chris Haddad, Wes Harrison, Brian G. Johnson, Dan Kennedy, Ben Littlefield, Mike Long, Wil Mattos, Zane Miller, Vivek Narayan, Eben Pagan, Justin Popovic, Brad Scott, Mike Stewart, Robert Stukes, Peter Wray, and Joey Xoto.

I've absorbed ideas from each of them. Frankly, I've been learning about marketing and marketing videos for years, and it's impossible for me now to remember who taught me what. If you are interested in learning from any of these teachers and have no luck doing an online search for their courses or books, if you email me perhaps I may be able to point you in a fruitful direction.

Nobody except me, of course, is responsible for any errors in this book.

Contents

Publisher's Notes

Preface

You know how it's often frustratingly difficult for small business owners to grow their businesses?

What can be done about that?

If you are trying to grow your business and avoid the top 40 marketing mistakes listed in this book, you will find that challenge much easier to overcome.

I assume that (1) you are in business selling your product or service in order to attract and keep customers, clients, or patients and (2) that you want to do this well in order to be at least financially rewarded for your efforts. If those assumptions apply to your situation and you are not already an expert marketer, I recommend reading this book in order to understand some major obstacles that could be preventing you from serving others better or becoming rich.

Please notice four initial points.

First, I assume that you are a one man gang, in other words, that you are your company. Whether that's true or not makes no difference; it's just for ease of presentation. Whether you work alone or have, say, fifteen full-time employees is irrelevant. If you hire employees, encouraging them also to read this book may benefit both them and your business.

Second, statistical generalities apply to populations rather than to individuals. You either make a mistake or you don't. Forget thinking in terms of odds or probabilities. As you go through the list, if you notice a mistake that you don't make, congratulate yourself, resolve to continue avoiding it, and move on. If you notice a mistake that you make, decide whether or not it's worth correcting or avoiding and, if it is, change your behavior from then on.

Third, the list of mistakes will be much more useful to you if you don't simply read it straight through quickly. For example, I hope that you are in the habit of giving yourself some quiet time each morning. If so, perhaps while sipping a cup of tea or coffee, why not consider one mistake each morning for the next forty mornings? Absorb each one fully and, if appropriate, begin to implement corrective action the same day that you consider it.

Fourth, since this is not an ordered list, read it in whatever order you prefer. If you are primarily interested in video marketing, you may want to begin by considering those mistakes specific to making and using marketing videos.

The outcome I'd like is simply for you to avoid (or continue avoiding) the forty mistakes.

Some mistakes you may not be making. Some may be relatively easy to correct. Some, though, may be difficult to correct; if that happens, I encourage you to get some help from the right kinds of people.

I wish you well.

1: Failing to Detach

If life is worth living, and it is, it's worth living well. Sages, those who live well, have let go of egocentric attachments.

I make no apologies for the fact that I have been a philosopher for over half a century. By definition, a philosopher is a lover of wisdom. Not everyone is a philosopher; sadly, some people fail to become philosophers and, because becoming wise is neither automatic nor natural, thereby condemn themselves to living without wisdom. Other people become philosophers and fail to become wise; their quest is unsuccessful. Sages, successful philosophers, become wise (and therefore cease to seek wisdom). The purpose of philosophy is to live wisely, to be wise.

What is it to be wise? As I think and talk, it's to live well. Are you seriously interested in living well? If not, you should be. Why? Obviously, the only alternative is not living well. Why would anyone not want to live well?

I taught undergraduates philosophy (and humanities) in the classroom for 32 years. Many who were 18 or 19 years old found themselves taking a philosophy course for the first time. It was always gratifying to me to learn the reaction that many had after the first class: they were already philosophers but didn't realize they were. Perhaps you are a philosopher without thinking of yourself that way.

Perhaps the most endearing quality of first or second year college students is their honesty. Once they trust you, they will often readily admit to being dissatisfied (discontent, ill at ease, unbalanced, suffering, confused, unhappy). The first step to ending

5

suffering is to admit that you are suffering. They lacked answers to the existential questions and realized that.

The existential questions are important questions such as: Who am I? Where did I come from? What should I do or be? What will become of me?

If you have ever seriously wondered about the answers to such questions, you have philosophized. You already understand that not understanding those answers hurts; such ignorance is at least uncomfortable and sometimes intolerable.

How could life not hurt if you don't understand its purpose or how to live it well?

What characterizes sages? What are those who live well like? These are important questions. I've never been able to understand why everyone is not interested in at least understanding living well. Why isn't everyone a philosopher?

My view is that sages have largely dropped egocentric attachments. In other words, sages live detached lives.

I have argued elsewhere for this view [see, for example, my Mastery in 7 Steps or Getting Things Done]. It is, of course, not an original view; some sages have been articulating it at least since the Axial Age about 2400 years ago.

What, you may be wondering, has any of this to do with marketing?

The answer is counter-intuitive. Although it initially seems irrelevant, it is not only relevant, but it is critical. Why?

If you are unable to understand how a prospect for your product or service thinks, you will always be, except accidently, unable to market effectively. No effective marketing, no successful business.

If you are unable to detach from your own egocentricity, you will never be able to understand the thoughts or conversation that is ongoing in a prospect's head. If you are unable to understand that, you will not be able to engage with what that prospect is already thinking about. If you are unable to relate to the thoughts a prospect already has, you will not be able to present your product or service, your offering, to that prospect effectively.

It's in marketing as in life: nothing is more important than detaching from egocentricity. There's no living well without it; there's no marketing well without it.

2: Expertitus

'Expertitus' is 'having the mindset of an expert.' What's wrong with that? When it comes to marketing, everything.

Marketing is about getting the right kind of people to pay attention to your message. Because not everyone will be interested in your message, it's important to select the right audience. Not every human being is a prospect. If you sell <u>Bibles</u>, you'll go bankrupt trying to make a living selling them to Muslims.

Even if you get your message in front of the right kind of people, they may not pay any attention to it. Each of us is bombarded by thousands of messages daily. It's impossible as well as undesirable to pay attention to all of them. We all filter out ones that don't interest us. We are predisposed to accept information that is aligned with our filters and predisposed to reject information that is misaligned with our filters. This is why not living an examined life obstructs us from reality.

What's your favorite topic of conversation? You! Your life and what's relevant to it, right? It's the same for prospects; they tend automatically to filter out anything that isn't obviously relevant to their lives. They value something when it's personally important to them.

[Since their self-understanding is almost always limited to the point of delusion, the range of what they value is miniscule. Instead of identifying with other objects, including other sentient beings and even other humans, they think of themselves as separate. This ego-delusion is the underlying precondition for our stunning cruelty to "others." One way to fight this tendency in yourself is always to try to judge "I am that"

9

when encountering objects that initially appear to be other.]

Well-qualified, certified experts have justifiable confidence when it comes to their subject matter. For example, I was a philosophy professor. I am a certified expert in the sense that I have a doctorate in philosophy (and my dissertation director has been recognized as one of the most outstanding contemporary philosophers). Furthermore, I happen to be very bright [a former member of MENSA] and, as the author of many books, articulate. When I taught a class, I didn't ask students what they wanted and then try to give it to them. Although I tried (usually poorly!) to relate the subject matter to their interests, I didn't really care what they thought about the core philosophical disciplines of ontology, epistemology, or axiology. Their relevant thoughts, if any, were, to put it kindly, unsophisticated. Instead, I attempted to teach them the relevant arguments from the appropriate philosophical dialectic.

This is why college professors are paragons of expertitus. Unless you are interested in their personal lives or desire a lecture about their subject matter, it's best to avoid them. In addition to suffering from common, nearly ubiquitous ego-delusion, they tend to be arrogant, annoyingly competitive, and status driven. (Kierkegaard's evaluation was on the right track.)

When those who suffer from expertitus attempt to create a product or service to sell in the marketplace, they tend to focus almost exclusively on creating products or services that they think would benefit people while paying little or no attention to what people actually want. The greatest sin of a capitalist is to ignore demand.

Introspect. Ask yourself, "Do I suffer from expertitus?" If so, cure yourself.

The way to cure experititus is to become a marketer, to adopt the marketing mindset. What's that? It's to focus on creating and promoting products or services that people actually want.

The great advantage of the marketing mindset is that it's much more profitable than suffering from expertitus. The chief reason for that is that it starts with reality. If there is little or no demand for a product or service, don't create it or have it created. If there is an unsatisfied thirst for a product or service, slake that thirst by creating it and offering it to those who are thirsty. [I point out its great disadvantage in # 6.]

There's nothing wrong with being an expert. If you are an expert, congratulations! However, if you want a successful business, take off your expert hat and replace it with your marketer hat.

It's difficult to overemphasize how detrimental to business success expertitus is. Perhaps the chief reason that I myself have struggled in business is that, even though I retired from the academy years ago, I still tend to think of myself as a philosopher rather than as a marketer. Like many professionals, my father had a similar problem. He was a board-certified internist and always thought of himself as a physician -- never as a businessman.

None of the suggestions in this book are categorical. I do not, for example, suggest that you never become an expert. That would be silly in an obvious way: if you never became an expert about something, how could you feel really good about your life? Instead, please take all the suggestions here to be hypothetical: *if* you want a successful business, *then* focus on marketing (rather than being an expert on any subject other than marketing).

In fact, when you get help running your business, the last duty to be outsourced to others should be marketing. It's too important to the success or failure of your business. Always stay focused on marketing. Hire experts about other subjects when you need help. [Cf. # 26.]

It's important to note that marketing expertise is itself never static. It's not as if one is able to learn marketing once and then use one's understanding profitably for the next fifty years. Since the marketplace is always changing, marketing that isn't also always changing is falling behind. This explains why, for expert marketers, marketing is a process.

A critical part of that process is testing. All good marketers are testers. Because the future is both unknown and unknowable, they understand that opinions about whether or not a marketing campaign will work are worthless. What matters is only what works. Marketers are pragmatists. The only way to determine what works is testing.

This feature makes marketing interesting as well as challenging.

Also, a test either works or it fails to work. A prospect either purchases or doesn't purchase. There's no third alternative.

Good marketers do not assume that a marketing campaign will work. There's no reason to assume that a prospect will purchase. In fact, most marketing campaigns fail; in other words, they demonstrate what doesn't work well. If one doesn't work well, so? Next. That attitude is characteristic of good marketers.

Therefore, if you happen to be an expert in something other than marketing, if you want a more successful business, please take off your expert hat. Detach from your expertise and focus on becoming a more effective marketer. This leads to a third important mistake.

3: Failing to Maintain Focus

What's the worst mistake humans make? Failing to focus on present experience. Having an unfocused mind is permitting thoughts to run amuck, permitting reality to be obscured by a thick cloud of thoughts. If so, it follows that correcting that mistake will be the single best strategy for improving your service to others and any business built on that service.

As I argue in multiple other writings, dissatisfaction (discontent, unhappiness, suffering) is always caused by separation. If your lover dies, you may become grief-stricken because you fully realize the agony of lasting separation. If you lose your house to foreclosure, forcible separation from your most valuable property may be very distressing. If you lose your job, everyone knows the intensity of the stress that may cause.

Our lives are unsatisfactory to the extent that we fail to heal separation.

Very often, it is attachment to certain thoughts that creates separation. The more I miss my family on the outside when I'm serving a prison term, the more suffering I create for myself.

We make a great advance in understanding how to live better when we realize that most of our thoughts are about the past, the future, or elsewhere. Life is here, now; it's impossible to live at another time or place. The present moment is of critical importance. Actually, there are no other moments because, as mere sets of thoughts [rememberings or imaginings] both the past and the future are nonexistent. The more we think about the past, the future, or elsewhere, the more we separate from life. This is why thoughts are so often hurtful.

I am not arguing, of course, that it would be wise never to think about the past. If we did that, how could we learn its lessons? I am not arguing that it would be wise never to think about the future. If we did that, how could we function in our everyday lives if we didn't plan future events such as obtaining food before eating or getting to the airport before the plane departs? I am not arguing that it would be wise never to think about what may be going on elsewhere. If we did that, how could we understand that we should help to feed the hungry in Africa or aid the drought victims in California?

I am claiming that most thoughts are useless and counter-productive. It's incessant, compulsive thoughts that are the problem. Some thoughts are unproblematic and useful; most thoughts are merely distracting us. [Cf. # 26.] It's not the mind that causes the trouble – it's our frequent misuse of the mind that causes the trouble. Since we need to solve problems, of course we need to think original, creative thoughts. It's not the 20% of fresh thoughts that create dissatisfaction, it's the 80% of stale, repetitive, useless thoughts that create dissatisfaction.

To reduce separation and, therefore, dissatisfaction, reduce thinking (conceptualizing). For sages, thinking is like sleeping or eating: they do it only when necessary.

Focusing is not necessarily thinking. Focusing is simply paying attention. We don't need to think about a flower to notice and appreciate its beauty. In fact, the more we think about it, the more we conceptualize it as an expert botanist would, the more we obstruct appreciation of its beauty. So-called moments of zen are nothing but moments of alert, nonconceptual awareness. The more we let go of useless thoughts, the better we live.

Focusing is often just letting go of thoughts. If you are an expert dancer, you don't think about dancing; instead, you just dance. You enjoy full engagement in

14

the present moment. It's only beginning dancers who have to think about what they are doing. In other words, to focus well is not to strain or to force concentration; it's simply to attend fully. If you are straining to dance well, you may be assured that you are not dancing well.

It's not only possible to improve focus, but it's simple (although not easy) to do so. I attempt to explain why this is so in books such as Mastery in 7 Steps and The Meditative Approach to Philosophy. I explain how to cure a lack of focus in more than one book; I provide instructions for zazen meditation in, for example, Love and Respect and for aliveness awareness in, for example, Emotional Eating. You can find, without spending a penny, instructions for both those kinds of training on my blog on living well [http://dennis-bradford.com/].

Experience has taught me that it's simply impossible to live well with an unfocused mind.

You have almost certainly had moments of full engagement. They may have happened during an emergency when it was critical to act rather than to think. They may have happened immediately upon waking up some mornings before the heavy avalanche of normal thoughts descended. They may have happened during some natural spectacles such as a thunderstorm, earthquake, or hurricane that temporarily stunned normal thoughts into submission. They may have happened during particularly intense sexual experiences. They may have happened in moments when noticing intense beauty killed thoughts. Such moments are natural and may be quite spontaneous.

On the other hand, if you are spaced out or lost in thought when writing an ad or conducting an interview to hire an outsourcer, the outcome you produce may well be inferior to what it could have been. For optimal performance, the mind must be trained (disciplined,

15

purified, concentrated). There is no optimal performance without focus.

The more thoughts are separated from behavior, the farther from the optimific or optimal your experience will be and, so, the more dissatisfied you will be. Whenever thinking has been replaced by alert, nonconceptual awareness of what is happening right here, right now, the more satisfied you will be. Living well happens when separation disappears.

Good marketers focus relentlessly on demand. If there's no demand for your product or service, nobody will purchase it and you soon won't have a business.

Good marketers focus on only the best prospects. Since most people are not the best prospects for your product or business, forget about them. Don't even worry about annoying them. The task of prospecting well begins with getting inside the heads of your best prospects, which requires letting go of the useless thoughts that are continually buzzing inside *your* head.

Who are the best prospects? What will you find inside their heads? Eben Pagan argues that they have four characteristics. Their demand is:

- So intense that it is emotional and, perhaps, irrational;
- So powerful that they are actively looking to satisfy it;
- So specific that there are few, if any, perceived options available to them; and
- Such that there is one concrete solution or benefit that will satisfy it.

4: Failing to Challenge Excuses

One of my occasional tactics when I was a college professor was that I'd hand out to all the students enrolled in a course a list of dozens of common excuses. I'd tell them that, for greater efficiency during my office hours, they should simply check the excuse they wanted to use and then hand me the list. (It was not a list I'd compiled myself. Another professor compiled it from actual excuses students gave him over the years for why they failed to perform excellently.) Students generally got the point, but there were some students who were exceedingly annoyed by that tactic. Apparently they felt deprived of the opportunity to come up with creative excuses on their own.

The more excuses you permit, the less successful or masterful you'll be. [I distinguish the success model from the mastery model in Part I of <u>Mastery in 7 Steps</u>.]

Sometimes, excuses are legitimate. If you break your leg and have to cancel that ski trip with your friend, let's hope that your friend forgives you. If you are running a fever, you shouldn't do strenuous exercise.

The problem, at least if you are like me, is that we are often too easy on ourselves. I'm tired, so I decide to take a nap instead of doing interval training. I have a cold, so I decide to skip my deadlift workout. I feel like watching a movie some evening, so I decide not to do formal meditation that evening.

If we discipline ourselves to do what we should do instead of doing what we feel like doing, even though that's difficult to do consistently, our lives improve; on the other hand, if we fail to discipline ourselves and consistently only do what we feel like doing, even though that's easy to do, our lives become more difficult.

For example, isn't it true that more first year college students flunk out than second, third, or fourth year undergraduates? Typically, they also gain pounds of body fat. What happens to them?

My guess is that many succumb to delusions about freedom. Beginning to live without their parents' supervision, they no longer have to study or eat or sleep the way that their parents used to try to get them to study, eat, or sleep. They relish for the first time what seems to be freedom. They think of themselves as able to study only when they feel like it, to eat whatever they want, to go to bed whenever they want, to use alcohol and drugs whenever they can afford them, and to have sex with the best partners they can attract.

That's not freedom; instead, it's merely slavery to desires. Genuine freedom is not freedom *from*, it's freedom *for*. This is an important reason why the value of a college education cannot merely be reduced to lifetime financial wealth accumulation. In fact, as I argue in Mastery in 7 Steps and elsewhere, living well doesn't require gaining anything; instead, it requires losing ego-delusion, letting go of critical egocentric attachments. It's the opposite of the way of the world, which is incessantly trying to gain what you want and to lose or avoid what you don't want. If all you do is follow the way of the world, all you are is a slave.

College is stressful. Learning better stress management skills than simply giving in to egocentric desires is an important lesson. Typical undergraduates lead interesting, hence stressful, lives. By way of contrast, typical graduate students lead more uninteresting lives that are much more tightly focused.

There's no genuine freedom without discipline. Anyone who remains a slave to egocentric desires is a slave. Learning that lesson is a mark of maturity.

Plato uses the analogy of a leaky jar that can never be filled [Gorgias 493]. Living a life of slavery to unceasing egocentric desires is like trying to keep a water jar full when the water is leaking out as fast as you pour it in. Why bother?

5: Looking for a Magic Bullet

Anyone reading this book is unlikely to be so immature as to believe that there is one magic bullet that will instantly cure all life's ills and that all we need to do to live well is to find it. Merely the idea that there are multiple, common mistakes just about marketing conflicts with the surrealties of those who think that all they would have to do to live well is to win the lottery.

There is no magic bullet. That's as true in business as it is in the rest of life.

Why?

It's because all success is temporal, spread out in time. There's no instantaneous success with respect to any valuable achievement.

It's true that successful people do frequently make success seem not only instantaneous but easy. What those who believe in a magic bullet approach ignore is the years of training that go into becoming successful even if one has the requisite ability.

How long does it take to become a great friend?

How long does it take to become a great quarterback in the National Football League?

How long does it take to become a great manager of a Fortune 500 company?

How long does it take to become a great pianist?

How long does it take to become a great parent?

How long does it take to become a great martial artist?

How long does it take to become a great surgeon?

How long does it take to become a great teacher?

There's no need to multiply examples endlessly. Many, many people who have achieved greatness have made the point that there is no magic bullet to any destination worth achieving. Even having the required native talent or ability, developing it to the level of greatness is never instantaneous. The very idea is ludicrous. It takes years of education and training. There's no substitute for consistent, disciplined practice of the right kind.

Yet we may still sometimes find ourselves hoping that success would come if only I could just land that client or seal that deal or obtain that loan. Not. When I notice that I'm idly dreaming, I realize that I am merely lost in thought. Idle dreams always have the form: "If only X, then Y." The if-only syndrome is a common affliction.

What can cure it? What helps when we simply find ourselves adrift and unanchored, dreaming idly?

My best recommendation is immediately to engage, even for just a short time, in a body practice such as aliveness awareness in order to get out of your head and back into your life. That's what I do. It also cures racing-mind insomnia. Since there's no better separation reducer, there's no better dissatisfaction reducer.

6: Lacking Integrity

Integrity in business begins with the product or service you are selling. Its quality must be good or excellent. What's the criterion for that? It's whether the solution you are offering the customer is worth more than the price the customer pays for it.

If possible, measure that in money. Assuming that the consumer uses it as intended, if the cost to a consumer is X dollars, will the benefits the consumer enjoys be worth at least X + 1 dollars?

If a consumer purchases your product or service and fails to use it, that's not on you. If, however, a consumer purchases it, uses it as intended, and fails to get more benefit from it than it cost, that's on you.

For example, suppose that you purchased a paperback copy of this book for about $10. If you never read it, you just wasted $10 and no blame attaches to me. If you read it and don't act on any of its recommendations, my hope is that your enjoyment of its prose was worth $10 to you. That is not, however, what I intended. My intention was to provide information that would help anyone interested in marketing, especially video marketing, who was not already an expert achieve more business success. (I assume that most experts would not be interested in a tips book.) The intended outcome was to provide you with information such that, when acted on, the benefit you would receive would be worth far, far more than $10. (Of course, there's no way for a seller to prevent someone's misuse of a product. For example, I am not responsible if an arsonist were to purchase a copy of this book and use some of its pages to start a fire that kills people.)

It's unlikely that any reader, even a marketing expert, even a video marketing expert, would already have been clear about all 40 ideas in this book. Any reader should be able to gain at least some understanding even if it's just one new idea.

There are ideas in this book that could be worth dozens, hundreds, or even thousands of dollars in increased revenue for your business if you execute them. Just one could be worth that. In other words, I believe that this book provides excellent value.

Another way to think about this is that it's often profitable to point out to prospects how you are selling more money than they are spending.

For example, suppose that you already know the value of video marketing and have been putting up videos on YouTube with the intention of attracting prospects. However, those videos are neither well-scripted nor well-structured. Furthermore, your videos were improperly set up on YouTube and your YouTube channel wasn't optimized. Depending upon the average lifetime value of a customer in your business, using the ideas in this book to fix just those four problems could easily result in tens of thousands of dollars of increased revenue just in the next twelve months.

Do I sleep well at night knowing that you spent less than $10 to purchase this book? Yes. I have a good idea what the information it contains is really worth.

Although it's impossible to quantify, I also hope that some of the ideas in this book stimulate you to live better overall and not just be more successful in business.

I don't know everything about marketing or even video marketing. Nobody does. If, though, I understand more than you do and am able to communicate some useful ideas to you that enable you to enjoy more business success, I'm expert enough to have benefitted you sufficiently. I neither pretend nor need to be more of an expert than that.

Integrity involves always trying to tell the truth. Say what you mean and do what you say.

The problem with truth telling is that it's impossible. Why? Judgments are always perspectival and, so, never the whole truth.

Judgments require concepts. Since concepts are principles of separation, they require classifying, sorting, categorizing, dividing, or discriminating. If I have the concept of a tree, I'm able to use it to separate trees from non-trees.

Concepts are tools. There's an indefinitely large number of ways to separate reality. There is no one way that works best for all purposes. Concepts are means to ends.

Since judgments require concepts and concepts require separation, judgments (conceptualizations) never capture reality as a whole. It's logically impossible. If we always stay stuck within conceptual systems, we condemn ourselves always to missing direct apprehension of reality. While concepts are useful, they are also misleading or obstructive. Reality is the conceptually obstructed obvious.

So, although it's important to try to tell the truth, actually telling the (whole) truth is impossible. Reality is greater than our thoughts about it.

Please, then, consider the top 40 marketing mistakes in this book merely as pointers. They are certainly not THE TRUTH. They are intended as fruitful tips or suggestions based on my experience. They are attempts to specify some partial truths.

Instead of believing any of them, instead of attaching to any of them, once you understand one, if you think it might be important for you, test it. If it works, terrific! If it doesn't, you'll at least have learned something that failed to work to improve your business.

That kind of skeptical attitude is characteristic of good marketers. Again, after all, the world is in incessant flux. Even if you test some of these ideas and they work, there's no guarantee they'll continue to work in the future. In fact, in 1 or 10 or 100 years, it's nearly certain that none of the more specific suggestions will work -- although I do believe that the more general ideas about living well will still resonate and be effective.

The great disadvantage of the marketer's mindset is that it is unrelated even to attempting to tell the truth [Cf. #2 and my It's Not Just About the Money!]. In the sense that it is sometimes financially counter-productive for marketers to tell the truth, there's nothing except morality that compels marketers to do it. Unfortunately, in that sense there are a distressing amount of immoral marketers who are, at least temporarily, financially successful. However, there are no good marketers who are immoral, who do not at least honestly attempt to tell the truth.

There are plenty of financial gurus who promote money-making as if it were an end in itself, as if having money were required for living well. While it's true that it's impossible to live well without having at least the resources to continue living, money is not a requirement for living well. In fact, lust after money has a very corrupting influence, which is why many spiritual traditions require poverty.

Whenever you find some marketer touting some money-making scheme without also talking about how it benefits others, consider that person as like someone who pushes addictive, nonprescription drugs that wind up harming their users. Such sickening marketers or drug-pushers may be financially successful, but they are immoral and I recommend avoiding them rather than emulating them.

If your product or service doesn't genuinely help someone live better, find another product or service to market.

7: Refusing Help

This one doesn't apply to you. Why? By reading this book you are already opening up to letting another help you.

The point, though, is not limited to general marketing education. It's also relevant to getting help running your business.

It's well understood that the skill set of a great entrepreneur who starts successful businesses is not the same as that of a great manager who runs successful businesses.

If you are starting your own business, there are very good financial reasons to delay hiring employees. Even if you happen to have an excellent method for hiring star employees, they always come with a high financial and psychological cost. Of course they need to be trained and supervised. Of course you hope that they'll be worth it, that they'll earn your business sufficiently more money than their costs.

The point is simply to delay hiring employees until you really, really need them.

What should you do if you need help and are not ready to hire either part- or full-time employees?

Hire independent contractors. For many tasks these days related to running a business, it's very easy to do online.

If you want to hire an outsourcer online, the procedure for doing so is neither difficult to understand nor difficult to execute. If you don't already know how, there are readily-available books and courses that are extremely helpful. For under $30, you can get up-to-speed very quickly.

I myself have hired Americans, Filipinos, Brits, south Asians, and eastern Europeans. I have hired both full-time and part-time contractors. Since I took the time to learn from experts how to do it before doing it, I've generally been quite pleased with the results.

I personally seem frequently to get stuck on technical problems. I excuse myself! After all, at 70 years old, I did not grow up with computers. Always, often for just a little money (e.g., $5), I am able to hire a contractor online to get me over a technical obstacle.

Whether you need a logo or a book cover or having a problem fixed on a website page, often for a few dollars or sometimes for a few hundred dollars, you'll be able to find a solution online. This is a wonderful opportunity that didn't exist just a few decades ago. Why not take advantage of it?

Furthermore, help is easy to train. [See the next suggestion.]

Don't neglect free help either. When you are lacking a demonstrable skill, instead of hiring someone else to do it for you, sometimes it's worth learning how to do yourself – especially if it's a skill that you will need again in the future. If you look online, you may be able to watch, for free, an expert's video demonstrating how to solve a problem. It's marvelous to be able to look over someone's shoulder as that person demonstrates what is, for us, a new skill.

There are, of course, often online courses and membership sites that relate to internet marketing. What I have learned about online video marketing I learned from my own experience that came from doing what some online expert recommended.

Your own experience is *not* the best teacher. Why? It's often very expensive and not just financially. Why not start any project by learning from the failures and successes of others?

If that's what you are doing with this book, good for you!

28

What's the worst mistake with respect to hiring help? I'm not sure, but my guess is that it's to hire technical help when you should be hiring marketing help. It's easy to hire technical stars to solve technical problems. If that's what you intend, that's fine. However, if what you really want is business growth, be sure to hire an expert marketer rather than an expert technician.

8: Not Using Videos to Train Help

This is a very simple tip that will increase efficiency and reduce aggravation.

Even if you don't currently have any employees or independent contractors to help you, why not now plan to become so successful you'll need help?

Why not make training that help as easy as possible?

Showing beats telling.

This is especially true if you happen to be training a contractor or employee and that person is not a native English-speaker. I've made the mistake of writing out lengthy verbal descriptions of exactly what I wanted done and given them to bright, hard-working Filipinos who were nevertheless initially unable to understand exactly what I wanted done. Duh! I should have used a video to show them exactly what to do instead of verbally describing in English what I wanted done.

You'll probably end up hiring help to do tasks for you. As soon as you now understand how to do a task, I suggest making a video recording of it and saving that video somewhere where you store all your instructional videos (such as Amazon S3 or Dropbox). When you do eventually hire help, simply give that helper access to those training videos.

Furthermore, if you now hire a contractor to do a technical task for you that you predict you'll need done again, ask that contractor up front to shoot a video of him solving the problem. You may be surprised to find that many will do that for you and not even charge extra for it.

If you don't know how to do something yourself and hire someone else to do it for you, it's very difficult to supervise their work. With the right attitude, it's fun to learn how to do new tasks. If it's a task that your business requires to be repeated, why not learn how to do it yourself, make a video recording of your doing it, and then from then on hire someone else to do it for you and use that video to train that person? This procedure won't work for all tasks, but it may work for more than you think.

Don't make the mistake of waiting until you hire help to begin making the videos. When you master a task and it's fresh in your mind, record yourself doing it. Even if you never hire any help, if months go by and you yourself forget how to do it, you'll be able just to watch the video to remind yourself how to do it. I learned this lesson the hard way. I'd master some technical computer skill, not use it for a year or two, and then find myself needing to do it again. Meanwhile, I'd forgotten the details of how to do it correctly and would, in effect, have to learn how to do it all over again. That's highly inefficient.

It's true that this tip will be more applicable to some skills than others. If you are doing a task on a computer, you may be able to use screen-capture video to record it. If you don't own and cannot afford software like Camtasia, as long as you limit video length to five minutes, you can use Jing, which is free. You'd just have to break up a longer process into shorter chunks for training.

YouTube contains many helpful videos on how to do various tasks. That's a terrific free resource for you or for your help.

If you want to record something that isn't merely capturing what's on a computer monitor, you may already own a camcorder, webcam, camera, smart phone, or an iPad or some other kind of tablet that may work perfectly well for your training videos. If you don't have a tripod or your project cannot be shot using a tripod, perhaps you could have a friend shoot you doing it.

In short, videos have important uses with respect to running or growing a business. It's a mistake to not to take advantage of that fact.

9: Not Attempting to Establish a Business Friendship

Since establishing a business friendship is much easier for a small business than a large one, doing so can be a great advantage that a small business has over a large business. Do you even know *any* large businesses that try to establish business friendships with their customers?

Suppose that you are speaking with prospects for video marketing. A good tactic is to compare your company to, say, the Yellow Pages. It's not just that the return on investment (ROI) for yellow page ads in the phone book is typically terrible these days, but it's also that that prospect is little more than a number to the Yellow Pages while he or she may be an important client for your small business.

Harvey MacKay and Eben Pagan are both business teachers who are known for stressing the importance of establishing personalized business relationships.

It's important to understand that most human beings have very little direct contact with reality. Instead, their encounters with reality are mediated, obscured, and obstructed by a thick cloud of conceptual filters. Instead of perceiving what is really there and then conceptualizing it, they literally perceive what they think is there. Since this has now clearly been established by psychological experiments, there's no controversy about it. We are all tainted by cognitive blind spots as well as by cognitive biases.

In other words, except possibly for some sages (I don't know because I'm not yet a sage), we humans live in our own surrealities rather than in reality.

It's important for you as a marketer always to keep this in mind. Since you are addressing your prospect's surreality or model of reality, you can forget about reality. The key to communicating your marketing message effectively is to let go of your own surreality as well as any direct acquaintance you may have with reality and to enter your prospect's surreality.

You already understand the product or service you have to offer. The idea behind a business friendship is to create an ongoing relationship with a prospect and then relate your offering to that person's situation. What does your prospect want? What does your prospect need? Is there a mutually beneficial match with what you offer?

The best way to find out is to have a conversation. Learn to ask and listen. Pay attention to what your prospect says and does.

Most people have an important problem: they feel that nobody really listens to them and that therefore they are really alone. Simply by taking the time to listen, you will decrease your prospects' feelings that nobody listens to or understands them. It's often repeated that prospects are more likely to do business with people they know, like, and trust than with other kinds of people. The more you listen, the more you genuinely care about what's good for your prospect, the more likely that prospect will either purchase from you or refer others to your offering.

It may seem that talking a lot to a prospect is the best way to establish a business friendship. It's not. The best way is to talk much less and listen much more.

Taking control of a conversation doesn't mean talking more. He controls the conversation who asks the questions whose answers form the bulk of the conversation. So, ask. [Cf. #11.]

Ask about your prospect's biggest relevant problems or frustrations. Ask about the implications of those problems, in other words, about additional difficulties that arise from not having effective solutions. Ask about what outcomes your prospect wants. Ask about the benefits of achieving those outcome. Finally, suggest the next step for your prospect to take and why you suggest it.

The trick to having that conversation well is to turn a negative into a positive. A good prospect for your offering has a problem, which is a negative situation. Direct your prospect's thinking towards a specific solution. Then ask the prospect to consider what he or she would need to achieve that specific solution. It's really powerful if you ask something like: "What ability do you have that you could use to achieve that?" Instead of a prospect's remaining mired in negativity, facilitate a transition that leads to a positive outcome.

It need not take much extra time or effort on your part to create a business friendship. Doing so will not only differentiate you from many of your competitors, but also it will benefit you as well as your prospect.

10: Not Leading with the Giving Hand

How do we create friendships?

Eben Pagan thinks that, typically, we begin with a commonality that enables us to generate rapport with someone else. Continued conversations and other shared experiences naturally lead to emotional connections. Emotional connections lead to committed behaviors that may become friendships.

Suppose that I sell fishing tackle. I offer to give you a lure. If you are not a fisherman, you won't take that bait. However, if you are, you may not only be open to receiving a free lure, but may come to value it if you use it. Suppose that I follow-up with some messages about fishing and we get talking. Maybe we share a cup of coffee while chatting about fishing. Eventually, we may even go fishing together and become fishing buddies. If that happens, where do you suppose you are going to buy fishing tackle?

That's the idea behind online lead generation. [Cf. #22.] You sell X and offer to give me something that I may value related to X without any cost or obligation in exchange for being able to contact me in the future. If I agree, you continue to try to connect with me in order to develop an ongoing business friendship that is mutually beneficial.

What needs to happen for that to occur is for you to bribe me in an ethical way to obtain my contact information. Once you have it, you use it to send me messages that you hope will hook me into wanting more from you. If you are successful, I purchase something from you and that may be the start of an ongoing business relationship.

This system works best if you give me something that I really value. Instead of just offering to give me a fishing lure, you might offer to give me information about how to become a more successful fisherman every time I go fishing. That valuable information may be given in various forms such as online videos or downloadable reports or books.

The chief point here is that you as a marketer should seriously consider simply giving away something that would be valuable to your prospects. That's an effective way to begin to establish a business friendship.

Part of why it's effective is because of reciprocity. If you give me something, I may feel an obligation to give you something back by purchasing something. To work effectively, the exchange may need to be more subtle than that, but what's critical is your gaining influence over me by giving me what I perceive to be a valuable gift. The more valuable I consider the gift, the more influence over me you'll normally gain. (Of course, if it's too valuable, I may refuse to accept it for just that reason.)

This is a standard way of attracting leads online. If you are not already using it, you should be. For example, when you put up a web page or an online video, consider using an opt-in box so that prospects can self-identify themselves as people who want more from you. Similarly, think of books (like this one) as lead generation machines. [Cf. # 24.]

11: Not Having a Customer Avatar

If you try to be all things to all people, you'll wind up being nothing to anyone. Again, not all human beings are good prospects for your offering.

Focus on identifying an ideal prospect who will become a customer. Do some brainstorming and research to create a profile or "avatar" of that prospect. Name him or her. Think hard about that avatar in the way that a good novelist would think hard about an important character in a story.

Here's a good research method. Find the websites of a few of your top competitors. Copy and paste the URL's of those websites into quantcast.com., run it, and then scroll down to learn the psychological and demographical characteristics of their visitors. Since they are already successfully marketing to people like that, ensure that your avatar has many of those same characteristics.

Then, and this is very important, always address your marketing messages to that avatar. Speak to one person and to one person only, namely, that avatar.

Since it's a common name that can be used for persons of either sex, let's here use 'Chris.'

Answer all the questions like these that a novelist might think of with respect to creating a character in order to create the best customer avatar for your offering:

Which sex is Chris? How old is Chris? Where was Chris born? Where does Chris live? Where has Chris lived in the past? What is Chris's background in terms of formal education? What is Chris's interpersonal background in terms of parents, siblings, lovers, and offspring?

What are Chris's habits? For example, is Chris a reader? How does Chris learn best?

What does Chris look like? What was Chris's self-image growing up? What are Chris's dietary, exercise, and, if any, nonprescription drug habits? How is Chris's health?

What does Chris most fear? What does Chris find most frustrating? What gives Chris the most physical pain? What does Chris worry the most about? What keeps Chris awake at night? Does Chris have any urgent problems? (It's very important to relate to Chris's dissatisfactions or pain points.)

What does Chris spend most waking hours doing? Does Chris have a job? What is the source of Chris's income? Is Chris affluent or hurting for money?

What does Chris most desire? What would Chris most like to do in life? What does Chris fantasize about?

What is Chris's surreality? What kind of world does Chris live in? For example, is it a world of abundance or scarcity? Is it a world full of fear or goodness?

Sleep on this. Refine you avatar over the next couple of days.

Most importantly, start to use Chris in your marketing.

For example, develop a specific elevator speech that relates to Chris. In general terms, where 'X' denotes an urgent problem that Chris has, it might go something like:

"You know how it's very frustrating to have to deal with X? Well, I solve that problem." Then, in one or two simple sentences, state specifically how you are able to solve that problem in a way that would really appeal to Chris. If possible, make it sizzle.

Offer Chris an ethical bribe in exchange for Chris's contact information. Then follow-up with messages written with Chris in mind that are designed to help move Chris towards a solution, which, of course, you offer. It's easy to follow-up online by using an auto-responder. You may write your follow-up messages in advance and load them into the auto-responder. Have a thank-you message with customer support details go out immediately after purchase. Follow-up with a helpful message a day or two later before Chris forgets who you are. The idea is to condition Chris to open messages from you because Chris has learned that they are beneficial.

12: Not Understanding a Prospect's Wants

What is Chris looking for? It's true that Chris is looking for a solution to a problem, but *how* is Chris looking for that solution? What would Chris really like to find?

It's fruitful to approach Chris's surreality from this direction. Here's the answer:

Chris wants to find someone just like Chris with one exception: that person has had the same problem Chris now has but has successfully solved it.

It's easier for us to know, like, and trust people who are like us than it is for us to know, like and trust people who are not like us.

This explains why politicians will sometimes present themselves wearing blue jeans instead of business attire: they are trying to encourage the average voter to identify with them. Of course, presidential candidates spend much more time fund raising than they do hunting or fishing and the average voter never spends any time fund raising. Appearances can be deceiving.

Is it immoral for politicians to present themselves as not being as they really are?

Look at it from the point of view of successful politicians. They have political power that average people never have. What really counts about a successful politician is whether or not that person leads people in such a way as to make their lives better. Everyone understands this.

Everyone also understands that to become successful, to get elected, a politician should present as appealing a face to the public as possible. If that means occasionally kissing babies, wearing Indian headdresses, driving tanks, or shooting quail, so be it. Yes, those kinds of activities are misleading, but what really matters is whether or not they are in the service of a good cause. Doesn't the end here justify the means?

Should you as a marketer try to appeal to Chris as if you were like Chris?

It ultimately depends upon whether or not your offering would be a good solution for Chris's problem. If it's a product or service that really will help Chris live better and it really does provide more value than it costs, then there's nothing immoral about your approaching Chris with your best face forward – and that face should be as appealing to Chris as possible. Make it as easy as possible for Chris to relate to you.

13: Not Having a Company Avatar

Your company avatar is the marketing face that you present to prospects. If Chris is your prospect avatar, your company avatar should be as much like Chris as possible.

Again, this is because it's easier for us to know, like, and trust those who we take to be like us than those who we don't take to be like us.

Like Chris, your company avatar is not a real person. Both avatars are imaginary. It's even possible to have company avatars that are appealing, even adorable, anthropomorphized animals or cartoon characters.

If the product or service you are offering would be an excellent solution for someone like Chris, both avatars are important for marketing purposes. Yes, a company avatar is deliberately deceptive, but it's like a white lie in the service of a good cause.

Furthermore, just as every voter understands that a politician's public image is deliberately created to make the politician more appealing, so every adult consumer understands that a company's avatar is deliberately created to make the company's offering more appealing. A lie isn't a lie if everyone knows it's a lie.

In developing your company's avatar, you'll want to answer many of the same questions asked about Chris in #11.

There is, though, an important additional consideration: what kind of approach will the company's avatar take towards prospects? If successful, the business friendship created will be a narrative, a story. What kind of story should it be? Decide. Test your answer.

The answer has two parts.

The first part of the answer is that it should be, or include, an enjoyable narrative. Ideally, it should be fun or entertaining. The reason is simple: we humans are predisposed to stories. We like them. They entertain us. We respond to them. We remember them easily. We use them to create our surrealities.

If both presented the same content, would you rather listen to someone telling you a story or someone lecturing at you? Other people are the same way.

It's always a good idea to do both: make a point and illustrate it with a story. Good public speakers do that all the time. If you just tell a story, people may miss its point. If you just make points, people will find them boring or less enjoyable than stories as well as more difficult to remember. The point is that "edutainment" trumps mere education. [Cf. # 32.]

The second part of the answer is that you should settle on one of three approaches for your company avatar. [I'm here following Frank Kern's suggestions from Eben Pagan's persuasion master class.] If it's not clear to a prospect which approach you are using or if you alternate among approaches, your prospect may get confused. Someone who is confused is stuck in a negative state and resistant to purchasing. A blended approach can be effective, but be careful if you use it.

What are the three approaches?

One approach is being a leader. The idea isn't to focus on being a leader; the idea is to focus on the problem the prospect has. Talk about that problem with authority and accuracy. The critical task with respect to this approach is to describe the problem even better than the prospect could describe it. If your company avatar does that, the prospect will automatically and naturally assume that what is being offered really is the desired solution.

Another approach is being a discoverer. What has your company's avatar discovered? The desired solution. The critical task using this approach is to tell the story of the heroic quest and subsequent discovery or fulfillment. Your company's avatar will become like a crusader telling the story of that often controversial or anti-establishment discovery. "Here's how I stumbled upon the secret to weight loss that physicians don't want you to know." The prospect is only still suffering from the problem because he or she has not yet heard the story.

Another approach is being a reporter. The company avatar used to have the same problem as the prospect. Often there was a loss of something valuable. However, and this is the critical task with respect to this approach, the company avatar then, fortunately, stumbled upon the method that more than redeemed the loss. The avatar isn't the hero – the method is. The narrative should be one worthy of an evangelist who happened to be at the right place at the right time and desires nothing more than to open the eyes of doubting others and convert them into true believers.

Remember that prospects may feel guilty about not yet living well, about still having an important unsolved problem. If you will absolve them from blame and alleviate their responsibility for their own condition (even if, in reality, they are responsible or partly responsible for it), you will encourage them to do what you say will help them. It's a bit like warming and relaxing a strained muscle in order to allow it to heal.

Credibility is usually enhanced if you don't make your company avatar or offering too good or too perfect. Making a damaging admission about one or the other or both often increases credibility. After all, nobody is perfect and it's difficult to identify with someone who seems perfect.

14. Failing to Understand a Prospect's Process

What process do you go through when confronted with a problem? It may be broken down into five stages. Since it's likely that prospects go through the same stages, crafting your marketing messages should take into account at which stage of the process your prospect is likely to be.

The first step in solving a problem is recognizing and admitting the problem. An alcoholic needs to identify and admit the addiction in order to have a serious chance at recovery. Marketing messages aimed at prospects who fail to think of themselves as having a problem are likely to be quite ineffective; when they aren't doing something (e.g., eating well or exercising well) and probably don't want to do it, educating others about what they should do well enough to prompt them actually to do it is very difficult. We tend to grow comfortable in our habits and resist change. We don't like to admit that we have problems that require curing.

The second stage is looking for options. Do I have alternative solutions? If so, are some better suited to me than others? Marketing messages aimed at prospects in either the second or third stage should emphasize their advantages over other alternatives. A prospect has admitted the problem and is likely to reject some as too difficult or expensive or otherwise unsuitable.

The third stage is eliminating some solutions. A prospect hasn't yet settled on one alternative, but he has ruled out some alternatives as unsuitable. He's looking for one option that positively differentiates itself from the rest.

The fourth stage is selecting one potential solution. Marketing messages aimed at prospects in the fourth stage should make a solution as risk-free as possible. A solution should at least come with an unconditional, money-back guarantee. After all, if your solution really is well suited for certain prospects, why shouldn't all the risk be on you?

The fifth stage is testing the chosen solution. If your product or service works as advertised for the customer, excellent! If you have had the foresight to have begun to establish a business friendship with that new customer, why not follow up with related offerings? Marketing to customers is much easier than marketing to prospects. If your offering fails to work as advertised, you want to do everything possible to make the situation right with that customer. Find out what went wrong and, if possible, fix it and, minimally, refund the purchase price and thank the prospect for letting you know about its failure. Do everything reasonable to leave a good taste in that customer's mouth.

Knowing that you have had a dissatisfied customer is much better than having a dissatisfied customer who you don't know about and who demeans you or your product behind your back. You should be able to help a dissatisfied customer you know about, but you are unable to help a dissatisfied customer you don't know about.

Always position yourself (or your company's avatar or your company) as someone genuinely helping others help themselves.

15. Failing to Focus on One Prospect Action

Marketing messages should always be understandable by bright 12-year olds. Keep them simple.

It's easy to get overwhelmed by choices. Reduce the options you give to prospects to "yes" or "no." Keep it simple.

Do not provide a cafeteria of options. That creates the necessity for evaluating different options and that can be difficult and confusing to do. Especially online, if something is confusing or too much work, your prospect will be gone in a flash.

One of my brothers worked for some years in the Soviet Union several decades ago. He married one of his interpreters and brought her to the United States. At first, she seemed overwhelmed by all the choices when she went shopping. In fact, she reacted negatively. She'd ask questions like, "Why do there have to be so many shades of lipstick?" We family members quickly learned to try to avoid having her accompany us to the grocery or drug store. She could easily spend half an hour selecting a single item to purchase from the dozens of varieties. Fortunately, she did quickly adapt to what initially seemed to her to be a nearly overwhelming plethora of choices.

It's almost always better to offer only two choices. In some cases, however, it is advantageous to offer three. For example, if you sell search engine optimization, you may have 3 bundles of monthly packages (good, better, and best). However, please don't have 4 and, usually, 2 choices are more effective than 3.

As always, test. Avoid <u>a priori</u> marketing.

16. Selling or Telling instead of Teaching

Education is stealthy marketing. If you help prospects to understand their options well, you usually won't have to hard sell anything. Forget about learning lengthy sales closes. Teach them something useful and then let them buy.

Nor is it necessary to tell prospects anything. Lecturing is not excellent teaching. When I was freshly out of graduate school and teaching an introductory course to undergraduates, I'd often prepare so thoroughly that I'd go into class with 10 pages of notes to cover 50 minutes. I assumed that they'd easily grasp the basic ideas, and I concentrated on fleshing out the details. Do I have to tell you that only a few of the most excellent students appreciated what I was doing? Most students were simply intimidated and overwhelmed.

I soon learned not to go into a normal philosophy class with more than 1 page notes. I then cut that down to a single 3 x 5 inch card. Often I later never used any notes at all and tried hard to ensure that nearly everyone understood at least the basic ideas. When that procedure worked well, I could still manage to throw out enough interesting questions to keep excellent students interested without losing or intimidating most students. (I never, though, despite what some students told me, thought of myself as an excellent classroom teacher.)

The best setting for teaching isn't a classroom; instead, it's one-on-one.

The best method for teaching isn't lecturing or telling; instead, it's the Socratic method. The idea is to lead a student's own thinking and discovery. It's not possible economically to have teachers and students relate one-on-one, but that's really the best method.

It can be emulated online. This is one reason it's important always to craft your marketing messages to a single prospect. If a prospect reads an email or other message from you, ideally it should seem to that prospect as if it was written just for him. When a prospect watches a video you made, it should seem conversational, as if you were right in front of him in person just talking with him.

Furthermore, try to build on your prospects' experiences. Draw lessons out of them. Do not, for example, use analogies that are likely to be unfamiliar. If you don't keep your meaning sufficiently simple, some will take you to be arrogant.

Someone who is intelligent and well-educated will not feel belittled if your words are simple and clear. Reading or listening "down" isn't a problem. However, reading or listening "up" is a problem. If you talk over someone's head, that person will tend to resent you for it. Instead, encourage prospects to feel good about themselves. Draw upon experiences they are likely to have had. Encourage them to think for themselves. Do that, and you'll build trust. Fail to do that, and you'll alienate people.

17. Ignoring the Cone of Experience

What's the cone of experience?

The general idea is to make it as easy for prospects as possible to understand and remember your message. The more experience or sensory modalities a student is able to use, the superior the learning outcomes, which are behavioral changes. No behavioral change, no learning.

The cone of experience comes from Edgar Dale's work in the 1970's and is still being revised and used. Here are its current critical implications for marketers.

If a prospect reads a marketing message from you, on average that prospect will remember only about 10% of the content of that message.

Similarly, a prospect who hears an audio message will remember 20%.

A prospect looking at still pictures or images will remember about 30%.

A prospect looking at moving pictures as well as simultaneously hearing a related message will remember about 50%. <u>That's all the justification ever required for using videos in your marketing messages</u>.

Even more of the message will be remembered when students learn actively by themselves saying, writing, and doing.

Therefore, if your product or service lends itself to a demonstration and you enable a prospect to view a video demonstration in which you talk the way though it as well as visually demonstrating it, you are likely to have an effective marketing video. It'll really be effective if you get prospects to do something to learn for themselves.

There are, of course, differences among prospects. For example, when I read a nonfiction book, it was always to me as if I were having a conversation with its author. I am a questioning, engaged, skeptical reader. I used to assume that everyone else read books as I did. Wrong! I eventually learned that, in fact, most people do not read like I read. Generalizing from one's own case is always dangerous. [See # 21.]

The critical takeaway point is that enabling prospects to see a video is about five times more effective than merely having a prospect read something.

Whether it involves marketing or not, if you make it easier for people to absorb and remember your content by using videos, you'll educate much more effectively than if you only provide them with ads, reports, or books to read.

18. Skimping on Preparation

You, too, have learned this lesson the hard way, right?

I learned it years ago in the late 90's when I joined Ken Evoy's program for using websites to produce online income. It contained a ten-stage plan for proceeding. After reading it I built my first website. I was much more concerned about learning the technical parts than I was about learning the writing part. After all, I had had several books published and already knew how to write. So I ignored his training about how to write webpages.

That turned out to be a foolish decision. Why hire an expert to help you and then ignore his advice?

I proceeded to write the website as if I were writing a book. It never occurred to me that I was doing something wrong until a new friend brought me up short. She started to read its pages and couldn't believe what I'd done: she'd never read anything online remotely similar. For good reason! Under her gentle but firm criticism, I eventually deleted the whole site and, together, we built a new one that was much more effective. Eventually, we made over $2000 a month in AdSense income from it.

Today, it amuses me how I initially proceeded. At least I did something and eventually learned from my mistakes.

Instead of paying attention to all the training that was available to me about, for example, researching keywords and writing webpages, I simply wrote what I thought would be good for readers to read. [Cf. # 2.]

If you were now to go back and look at a single page of that site, you'd be appalled. It would have been a page dense with words. There were no images or videos. There was little white space. There were very long paragraphs. There were no outbound links either to pages of other websites or to other pages of that site. Even more incredibly, there was only one way to get to a page and one way to get off a page; in other words, you either had to read its pages in the sequence I determined in advance – like a book with each page in sequence – or you could not even get to a page!

My basic mistake was in assuming that writing a page for a website was like writing a page for a book. Not. It ignores the important differences, for example, between reading a computer monitor and reading a page of a physical book. It's much more difficult to read a paragraph on a monitor than to read a paragraph in a book.

So the rules for writing a web page are different from the rules for writing a page in a book. For example, paragraphs online should almost never be longer than 3 lines of text; there's no such limitation in writing a page in a book. For example, it's always best to have plenty of white space on a website page to alleviate eye strain; there's no such limitation in writing a page in a book. It's always a good idea to have a photo or other image on a website page. It's always a good idea to have an outbound link to an authority site on a website page. Because it may be the first page of a website that a visitor ever sees, it's always a good idea to write a web page in such a way that it may stand alone. And so on.

Doing keyword research to evaluate demand and competition before writing a single page was wholly alien to me. So I just skipped it.

The result was predictable. Except for my friend, I'm not sure that anyone else ever visited that website and, if others did, I'm sure they left almost instantly.

If you are going to write a web page or surf or ice skate or be a landlord or whatever, is it a good idea to make all the mistakes yourself or enlist help from an expert? Making all the mistakes yourself is usually as painful as it is time-consuming.

Slow down. Don't just fire without aiming. Think critically about a project before starting it and then do your due diligence. Would you buy an automobile without researching what other owners have discovered about that kind of automobile?

Even if you do decide to begin a project, keep researching it. Keep learning about it. Do not, for example, buy a single book on strength training and then slavishly follow its routines for the rest of your life. Keep learning from the experiences of other strength trainees as well as from your own experiences. Learning should be enjoyable, and learning what not to do is often even more profitable than learning what to do. Aren't you enjoying learning what not to do as you read this book?

What's the most important subject to research when considering entering any market niche? Demand. This leads directly to the next point.

19. Not Starting with an Assembled Crowd

Here's a familiar marketing question: "If you were considering opening a new restaurant, what's the single most important factor that would predict success?"

It's not location. It's not having a master chef. It's not having beautiful décor. It's not having a well-trained staff. It's not having a long menu full of delicious choices. It's not having low prices. It's not having fast service.

It's having a starving crowd.

Don't nearly all small start-up businesses fail within 5 years? A chief reason why is insufficient demand.

Here's one way to make some money online that's just an example of finding an already assembled crowd before you do much work or spend much money.

If you wanted to make money writing a book, how should you proceed? Wouldn't it be wise to emulate success? Go online to amazon.com and other places and investigate what kinds of books are selling well. Find a genre where there's lots of books being sold, which indicates lots of demand, and match that genre to your writing skills. If it's a good match, proceed. If it's not, select a different genre (or drop the project). Once you select a target genre, read 5 or 10 of the bestsellers from the genre and note their similarities. Is it realistic to believe that you could emulate them? If so, proceed. If not, find a different genre (or drop the project).

If you then proceed, figure out an effective marketing plan. Because it's nearly certain that you won't make much, if any, money if you do, I suggest that you avoid submitting your book to traditional publishers. Instead, take a couple of courses on how to make money writing books that you publish or have published. Then, using at least some of those similarities you found when reading, write your book. As you are doing that, develop an appetite for it among potential readers and, if it's your first time, be sure to get some help with your book launch.

Do you realize that you may be able to become an Amazon bestseller in certain niches by selling as few as 100 or 200 books in 24 hours online? Being able to identify your book as a bestseller increases social proof, thus encouraging sales. Launch your book and promote it properly. Do your best to have it become a bestseller. Absorb the lessons learned. Was it worth it? If so, repeat the process again. Persist until you are as successful as you want to be or until you decide to do something else.

I'm not, of course, saying that you should write a book with the intention of making money from its sales. I'm saying that you should consider demand before you go into any business venture. [I do, though, suggest that you should do a book for another reason; see #24.] If you want money and there's insufficient demand with respect to some contemplated project or other, do something else.

Furthermore, of course, don't do a business project of any kind unless it's a good match for your skills. If it is a good match, don't worry too much if you are not overly enthusiastic about it initially. Why? If it suits you, your passion for it will tend to grow as you work at it and become better at it.

If you wind up with a project that combines demand, your talents, and your enthusiasm, you are much, much more likely to be successful than otherwise.

20: Insufficient Testing

Successful marketers are testers. Test everything important about your marketing.

Details matter. It's amazing how much they matter. If you read books or websites by marketing or advertising gurus, you'll find plenty of stories of how one little tweak made an enormous difference in sales.

Fortunately, it's easy to test online marketing. There are different ways to test, but simple split-testing that's repeated is often good enough. Marketing does not have to be perfect; it only has to be good enough. [Also see # 26.]

It makes no difference whether you are writing ad copy or email messages, whether you are choosing fonts or colors, whether you are using talking head videos, presentation videos, or animated videos. Test.

Why?

Common sense simply doesn't work. Using common sense, it's impossible to predict what will work.

Furthermore, everything is contextual. Suppose that you test, for example, a landing (squeeze) page with respect to its background color and you discover that red works much better than white or black or any other color. You may think, "Good. From now on I'll use red backgrounds on landing pages." Please don't draw such conclusions! Marketing isn't generalizable. The next squeeze page background color test you do for a different offering may determine that red is worse than white or black or any other color for its background. Sorry.

A simple, effective way to test is, ideally, to select the most important element and start with two widely different alternatives (usually called 'A' and 'B') of it. When you find which is better, test that one against a third alternative. Repeat until testing reveals not much difference between the alternatives and then select the next most important element and repeat the process.

What are the most important marketing elements to test? What are the least important elements to test, in other words, the ones that should be tested, if at all, only after you have tested the more important ones?

According to Jason Fladlien, the three most important elements to test about a landing page are, in order of importance, the design or layout, the price, and the headline. Unfortunately, the headline is the easiest of the three to test, the price is the next easiest to test, and the design or layout is the most difficult to test.

What should you test about the design or layout? Its background color always makes a difference. Should it be a solid or a pattern? Should it have a gradient? Should it be visually simple or rich? Next check the fonts and font sizes of both the headline and body text. Also, should there be an image or a video? If the image is of a person, should it be male or female? If there's a video, what kind should it be?

What should you test about the price? Obviously, test different prices. Although common sense might predict that lower price would always win, that's false. Also, is it better to have a payment plan? If so, does a plan with two payments work better than three payments? Should there be a trial offer in addition to a full pay offer? Are there wide differences in refund rates?

What should you test about the headline? Does a short, powerful one work better than a long, descriptive one? Does a positive one that emphasizes a benefit work better than a negative one that emphasizes lack of a benefit or pain point?

Don't always be afraid to experiment. While experiments that break the usual rules often fall flat, they can also be wildly successful.

After you have split tested the design, price, and headline and they are working well, then go on and test such more minor elements as the order button color, load speed, images, and order form text.

It's possible to research split testing at various websites. I use the Thesis framework on some WordPress sites and that's one place to go: http://diythemes.com/thesis/increase-conversions-split-testing/ Another is the blog at http://www.zentester.com and there are many more.

Only you can determine how much testing is sufficient. At least test the major elements of any online marketing campaign and do not assume that such testing results apply to other marketing campaigns.

21: Assuming that Others Are Like You

I alluded to this mistake in #17 where I mention my false assumption that others read books as I do. That kind of mistake is a natural one to make. Once we realize it, we open ourselves to relating to others better.

Education is the ultimate stealthy marketing. If you will position yourself in the marketplace as an educator who wants to help others help themselves and market accordingly, don't be surprised when your business grows.

The most important mistake that you as an educator can make is to assume that others are like you in terms of their learning style. Some really are like you, but most are not.

In his "Guru Bootcamp" Eben Pagan argues that there are 4 learning styles and that the best way to teach an independent idea is to remove the obstacles to understanding it that obstruct people who have different learning styles. Imagine that there are 4 different kinds of students in your classroom and ensure that none of them is obstructed from learning what you are teaching. The goal is to make it as easy as possible for all 4 different kinds of learners to learn.

Actually, each person is a combination of each of the 4 learning styles. It's quite helpful, however, to distinguish each of the 4 in terms of their chief obstructions. If you will remove each of the 4 kinds of obstructions whenever you teach, you will become a much more effective teacher. The best way to become a more effective marketer is to become a more effective teacher.

What are the 4 learning styles? What chief obstruction does each have? How can we as teachers remove those obstructions?

Someone who has a predominantly "why?" learning style always asks, "Why should I learn this?" Without having a clear motivation to learn, this kind of student is obstructed from learning. Therefore, always provide that motivation. Even if only briefly, explain clearly the good outcomes that will occur if the material is learned and the bad outcomes that may occur if it isn't. Whenever you are explaining or teaching something, be sure to help *why* learners get past their psychological block by explicitly providing the motivation. It's even beneficial to sprinkle motivation throughout the instruction. (Apparently about one-third of us are *why* learners.)

Someone who has a predominantly "what?" learning style always asks, "What am I learning?" Without understanding the context of the subject matter, this kind of student is obstructed from learning. People like this are abstract conceptualizers [like me]. They already enjoy learning and don't require motivation to learn. It's just that if they are disoriented they are blocked from learning. In other words they want to understand the philosophy, theory, history, psychology, and so on of the subject matter. Whenever you are teaching, simply ensure initially to put the subject matter in its context. (Most professional teachers as well as professors are *what* learners.)

Someone who has a predominantly "how to" learning style always asks for exercises and action steps. Without understanding the correct procedure (recipe, process), this kind of student is obstructed from learning. They are not initially interested in "why?" or "what?" Once they are able to follow the correct procedure, the "why?" and the "what?" fall into place for

70

them. They seek the exercises and action steps. Whenever you are teaching, always provide specific action steps to enable *how to* learners to get what you are teaching. (Apparently about one-fifth of us are *how to* learners.)

Someone who has a predominantly "what if" learning style learns best by taking action. These doers are the world's entrepreneurs. They are the students who leave a course or convention midway through as soon as they decide that they have learned enough to take action; in other words, they are eager to apply what they learn. They are less interested in abstract understanding than practical results. They take action by implementing what they have learned, get feedback from it, adjust what they are doing, and do it better the next time. Whenever you are teaching, make it as easy as possible for *what if* learners to apply what you are teaching by offering concrete applications.

The takeaway lesson here is that, whenever you are teaching, explicitly, even if briefly in a single sentence, address each of the 4 obstructions. It doesn't matter whether you are giving a talk, writing a report or book, or creating a video. It is not necessary even to give each equal time. All that's important is quickly knocking down each of the 4 obstructions. Doing that will be received by each of the 4 kinds of learners as a personal invitation; it makes everyone feel welcome.

Since each of the 4 kinds of learning styles may have the same behavioral outcome, none is inherently better than the others. Each works.

If your own learning style is predominantly one of the four, your tendency will be to knock down only the obstruction that is important to you and to ignore the other three. If you want to market effectively as a teacher, that's an important mistake to avoid.

22: Failing to Build a List

Since many, many successful online marketers have emphasized the importance of building an email list, this may already be a familiar tactic to you.

This tactic connects with #10. Actually, it is the best online way to lead with the giving hand: give something with high perceived value to a prospect in exchange for that person's email address. (Opt-in rates are always higher if you simply require an email address rather than requiring both a name and an email address or asking a prospect to make a phone call.)

What you give may be inexpensive to you, but it should be valuable to a prospect. Don't you have a tendency to diminish the importance of what you yourself understand? Don't you have a tendency not to value your own understanding highly enough? Given your experience, something may now seem obvious to you that would be an extremely helpful revelation to a prospect. After all, in your field you are an expert. Most others, though, are not experts in your field.

The best gift is the gift of understanding. Why not create an information product such as a video that would be relatively easy for you to create and really helpful to someone who doesn't understand what you understand? Make a list of what are likely to be your prospect's three top problems. Which one could you best help your prospect solve at little cost to you?

Don't worry about giving away too much free information. You may fear that your prospect won't be inclined to purchase your offering if you have already given away some really helpful information. That's the opposite of what usually happens. Why?

It's the wrong psychology. The predominantly right psychology of your prospect will be: "If I'm getting this much help for free, just imagine how much more I could get if I purchased!"

Here's an important tip that I learned from Jason Fladlien: instead of simply giving away a downloadable report or video, give away a membership to a membership site. Why? Since membership sites are usually paid membership sites, giving one away has a high perceived value. Simply put your report or video inside the membership site – perhaps along with another helpful but unannounced bonus as well as a link or two to your paid offering(s).

A downside to this suggestion is that some software for building membership sites is expensive. However, if you would like a free membership site on a Wordpress platform, there are now available inexpensive plug-ins that will enable you to create one without much difficulty.

After you have a list of prospects, do follow-up with those who join your list before the list goes stale.

When a prospect transitions into a customer, put that person on a customer list. If you treat your customers like business friends, a customer list of even just a few hundred really can put thousands and thousands of dollars into your pocket.

Consider, too, enabling your business friends to benefit whenever they send you leads. Have a good lead referral system in place as well as a customer reactivation program. The best kind of marketing is word-of-mouth. In fact, it's often a very profitable idea to set up your own affiliate network for your offerings.

Since your lists of prospects and customers are very valuable to you, ensure that they are well-secured in multiple locations. If you ever lost all your assets except those lists, they may enable you to rebuild rather quickly. Since your lists can provide insurance against asset loss, they may help to provide peace of mind and should be really well protected.

23: Failing to Optimize Website Pages

It's likely that you or your business will have a website, which is a collection of online pages. If you are going to put up a website page, at least do its on-page optimization correctly. That means setting it up in such a way you enable the "spiders" sent out from the major search engines to crawl it easily.

Since the algorithms used by those search engines are frequently updated, even if I were able to tell you how to optimize a website page perfectly today, that information would be dated tomorrow. Think of optimizing website pages as an ongoing process.

That applies to both on-page and off-page optimization. This suggestion concerns only on-page optimization, but off-page optimization is at least worth considering when it comes to YouTube videos. Off-page optimization is all about building, or enabling others to build, backlinks to your online property. To the spiders, those links to your online properties such as websites, playlists, and videos are like votes. It's not just the number of votes that matters, it's also where those votes are coming from that matters. Just a few links from websites with a high domain authority can make a lot of difference in search engine rankings. Again, though, that is not our topic here.

A "keyword" is simply a word or phrase that someone types into a search engine. Some keywords are used much more frequently than others. A search engine results page (SERP) provides a list of online properties such as websites or videos for a keyword in order of popularity. If your online property is popular, it will be found on the first page of, say, the relevant

Google SERP. If it's in one (or more) of the top three positions, it's well-placed to direct traffic to your online property.

It's much easier to get an optimized website page highly ranked on relevant SERP's than it is if that page is not optimized. This is why it's a mistake not to optimize website pages. If you do the work to put up a page and nobody ever finds it, your effort was wasted.

Although neither is there now (partly because I have failed to keep up with optimizing their pages), I myself have ranked two websites in the top ½ of 1% of all websites, namely, lasting-weight-loss.com and dennis-bradford.com. When I put up a website page today, what follows is a list of the ten most important practices I follow. If you already have a website whose pages are not ranking as highly as you'd like, you'd be wise to optimize them in accordance with these practices and watch what happens to their rankings. From now on, whenever you put up website pages, I recommend that you follow these 10 practices (or updated versions of them).

Of course, if someone else is handling your business website for you, simply give that person this list. If you don't understand any of the technical jargon in the list, don't sweat it. Either just give the list to your webmaster or take sufficient time to educate yourself.

This is just one of many ideas in this book that, if implemented, might repay the cost of this book a hundred or a thousand times over.

The title of the web page should be the best keyword for that page.

The name of the page should also be the best keyword for that page.

The first H1 tag on the page should match the page's title.

Put a related video on the page. How? One way is simply to do a YouTube search using that page's keyword. Copy the embed code from the first video that appears and use that code to embed the video on your page. Just before the video, use the best keyword in an H3 tag to introduce the video using a phrase like "Video about _____" or "Check out this video about _____" and fill in the blank with your page's keyword. Another way, which may be more effective, is to put a video you made on the page.

Have links to your legal pages (e.g., terms of use, privacy policy, etc.) in your footer. It's best if the navigation in the page's footer is based on the best keyword. Create a link to the site's homepage in the footer.

Use both XML and HTML sitemaps for that page.

Any links from that page to other pages of your website should only go to other pages within the same silo. (Your site's content should have a silo structure, which is organizing its content into categories to make it easier both for human visitors and spiders to find the subject matter of its pages. If you are building a new WordPress site, there is now at least one relatively inexpensive plugin that automatically sets up a silo structure.)

Have at least one link from that page go out to an authority site and it should open in a new window. If nothing else, have the link go to Wikipedia or to a relevant site with a .edu or .gov suffix.

Have between 800 and 2000 words of original, high-quality content on that page that is directly related to the best keyword. It should read naturally and have a keyword density for the best keyword under 1% and LSI synonyms should be used.

Have a clear call-to-action (CTA) at the bottom of the page. Tell the visitor what to do next and give a reason for doing it. For example, "To learn more, complete and send this opt-in form."

24: Not Getting Your Conversion Book Done

If you are serious about growing your business, you should think of yourself primarily as a marketer rather than as a psychologist, plumber, attorney, or whatever. [Also see #2.]   Once you thoroughly adopt the mindset of a marketer, you will naturally begin to do what good marketers do.

What do good marketers do?

They spend about 80% of their business efforts attracting and converting traffic.   Everything else involved in managing a successful business should occupy the other 20% of a marketer's business efforts. [Cf. # 26.]

Attracting traffic is for acquiring leads. Many of the ideas in this book are suggestions about how to maximize your lead generation efforts. To get warm prospects, you need prospects. To get prospects, you need traffic. So the idea is to get lots of traffic in order to get lots of prospects in order to get lots of warm prospects. It's rather like wanting more quality time with your children. Do you want more quality time with your children? If so, spend more time with them. The more time you spend with them, the more quality time you'll have with them.

Traffic is not profits. For example, just because your online video is ranked #1 on a SERP does not mean that you'll be making lots of money.   To increase your income, you not only need more prospects, but you also need to convert more of them into customers, clients, or patients.

If you want to grow your business, those two tasks are what I'm recommending that you focus on.

Again, the purpose of a business is to attract and keep customers, clients, or patients. If you do that well, you'll make a profit. The more leads you convert into customers, clients, or patients, the more profit you should make. This explains why, if you want a more successful business, you should spend most of your productive time attracting and converting traffic.

Everyone understands (yet again!) that prospects want to do business with those they know, like and trust. A great way to do that is to do a conversion book. There is no faster method for improving your conversion rate than doing a well-constructed conversion book and using it properly. If you doubt that (and you should!), just test it for yourself. In general, once you are attracting lots of leads, there is no better way to increase your bottom line than increasing your conversion rate. In that sense, this may be the most important marketing mistake to avoid.

People don't want to do business with companies; they want to do business with people.

A conversion book is a book that you give to prospects with the intention of educating them, thereby benefitting them and indirectly encouraging them to get more from you. Although it's not selling, at least not directly, a well-done conversion book is extremely effective marketing.

A conversion book almost instantly boosts credibility. A well-constructed conversion book never fails to impress.

This process is so important that I have written a book about it, namely, How To Become Happily Published. If you don't have a copy, I encourage you to pick one up. [It's available from amazon.com. You can order a paperback or, for just $2.99, an e-book version.] It provides complete instructions on how to do your own well-constructed conversion book.

Notice 'do' rather than 'write.' To most people who have never done it, writing a book seems as gigantic a task as climbing a mountain. Well, thanks to modern technology, it's no longer even necessary to write a book to get one done.

I explain exactly how to get a book done even without writing it in How to Become Happily Published. I explain exactly how it's easy for an expert to produce sufficient content. You're an expert about your business, right? You already have the answers to the objections that prospects have. You already understand why your offering would be more valuable to your prospect than its price. It's really just a matter of making your understanding concrete.

Remember, if your book isn't short and to the point, most prospects won't read it. You want to make it a quick, informative, and enjoyable read. Believe me: you can produce all the content you'll need on a Saturday morning.

Once you have the content, get it edited. All that then remains is getting that content into a well-constructed paperback. (Since it's impossible to hand an e-book to a prospect, your conversion book needs to have physical form.) It's not difficult to get the book well formatted and it's easy to have a very nice cover produced very inexpensively.

Although having an attractive front cover is important, a critical element to the book's success as a conversion tool is to have the right kind of back cover. What should it be? It should be a formal headshot of your smiling face *accompanied by media logos*.

(If you want a good example of one of my conversion books, you may order from amazon.com a paperback copy of my 12 Publicity Mistakes that Keep Marketers Poor for under $10. Please pay particular attention to its brevity, clarity and covers. If you are reading this book as an e-book, you are able to see the photo that I used for it in black-and-white near the end of this book or, in color without the logos, at my Author Central page, which is at: http://www.amazon.com/Dennis-E.-Bradford-Ph.D./e/B0047EI11A/ . In paperback, the book you are reading is also a conversion book.)

The media logos are important with respect to your consulting book. Why?

Everyone recognizes them. When you hand a prospect your book, what will the prospect do? Look at it. He or she will look at its cover with your name on it and think, "Wow. This person is an expert." That person will also naturally flip the book over and glance at its back cover. The reaction? "Holy smokes! This person isn't just an author but a celebrity!"

When was the last time an author gave you a free book? Perhaps never. How would you feel if an author did? How would you feel if a celebrity gave you a book? How would you feel if that author also autographed it for you?

You'd feel as if you'd just met an important influencer. Not only would reciprocity immediately kick in, but because of the logos so would social proof. If you were then to read that book, you'd also be immensely impressed if it was not only clear and concise but packed with useful, actionable information.

Prospects react the same way. I've watched it many times.

When you hand out a copy of your properly constructed conversion book, you immediately heat up a prospect and so dramatically boost the odds that that prospect will convert to customer status. If that prospect wants your service or product, closing may be as easy as asking, "When do you want to get started?"

How much would getting a conversion book done cost? Nothing! Why?

Its initial price depends upon how you get it done. It could be as inexpensive as $200 or as expensive as $5000 or more. If you were to use my other book as a guide to producing the content, there's no reason why it should cost more than a few hundred dollars. [You can get more information at ironoxworks.com.] Remember, too, that's a one-time expense that should be tax-deductible. Once you have your conversion book in hand, you can use it for years. (If you ever want to update its back cover photo, that's inexpensive to do.)

How much would it cost initially to buy copies to hand out to prospects? Here there's really good news. It usually costs less than $2.50 per copy!

How could it be free if you spend $1000 to get it done and, say, $250 for a hundred initial copies?

Let's run some sample numbers. How much money do you make per average customer transaction? Obviously, that depends upon your product or service. Let's take an example. Suppose that you install granite countertops in kitchens and usually make $750 per installation. You spend $1250 on your book. If you assume a meager and unrealistically low 2% higher conversion rate the first year, you be ahead $250 (2% of 100 is 2 and 2 x $750 is $1500 less the $1250 initial costs). Until you needed to replenish your supply of copies to hand out, *it'd be nothing but pure, increased profit from then on.*

Think of it from a customer's point of view. Suppose that I am in the market for a new countertop and call you for an estimate. You come to my home and give me, in addition to leaving me a $5000 estimate, a properly constructed conversion book you did about mistakes to avoid when selecting kitchen remodelers. Your smiling face is on its back cover next to media logos from the big four national television networks. Don't you think I might hire you for the job even if someone else came in with a lower estimate? After all, I'm looking for a beautiful countertop without any complications, not necessarily a cheap installation. Who would be more likely the give me a beautiful countertop than a celebrity who wrote the book about kitchen remodeling?

If you haven't yet done a well-constructed conversion book, I strongly recommend that you do one and begun giving every good prospect a copy. If you don't, you are leaving money on the table.

25: Focusing on Traffic Too Early

What's the point of acquiring leads if you don't have your conversion strategy set up?

It doesn't make any difference whether those leads are coming from online or offline. If your conversion strategy isn't in place, you are wasting time and money generating traffic.

Suppose, for example, that I hire someone to do search engine optimization (SEO) for a video on my YouTube channel. In other words, suppose I hire someone to generate backlinks to a video in order to improve its SERP ranking. That's fine, and perhaps my video will land on the first page for its best keyword and perhaps even land in one of the first three spots in the organic (free – not paid) listings. However, if my video isn't properly structured to generate leads, the money I spent getting it ranked higher will have been wasted.

The same thing happens when I have a website page optimized off-page but fail to have it optimized on-page. That's backwards. At least ensure on-page optimization [see # 23]. It may not even need off-page optimization. If it does, it may not need much off-page optimization.

It makes no sense to put the cart before the horse. Get your conversion funnel set up and then work on filling it with traffic.

That especially includes getting your conversion book done. [See #24.]

26: Ignoring the 80/20 Principle

What's the 80/20 principle?

"The 80/20 Principle asserts that a minority of causes, inputs, or effort usually lead [*sic*] to a majority of the results, outputs, or rewards ... there is an inbuilt imbalance between causes and results, inputs and outputs, and effort and reward" [Richard Koch, The 80/20 Principle: The Secret to Success by Achieving More with Less].

Like many success principles, this is counter-intuitive. It seems to be commonsense that there's a balance between effort and reward, so that the greater the effort, the greater the reward. Not. Most likely there's not only an imbalance, but a surprisingly great imbalance.

It doesn't have to be 80/20. It could be 90/10 or 70/30 or 75/25 or whatever. (My recommendation in # 24 to spend 80% of your business efforts on generating and converting leads is to be understood in a heavily imbalanced – rather than precise – way.) In other words, like chaos theory, the 80/20 principle is grounded in nonlinearity. It's explained by, and obviously consistent with, the idea of feedback loops, which I have discussed elsewhere [see Personal Transformation].

Everyone who is successful in business understands that differentiation is critical. If your product or service is not differentiated in a prospect's mind in a positive way from those of your competitors, why should a prospect purchase yours?

Good marketing is the sine qua non of business success. If you want to pull ahead of your competition, it's critical that you differentiate yourself as a marketer. How? Focus on the nonlinear relationships that many or most of your competitors are neglecting.

Which 20% of my offerings generate 80% of my profits? Identify those and focus on marketing them.

Which 20% of my business tasks generate 80% of my profits? I've identified them for you: those tasks that focus on generating and converting leads. Focus on attracting prospects and converting them into customers, clients, or patients.

Are you settling for inaction? Are you letting your excuses get in the way?

Judging by their behavior, most people fail to figure out the nonlinear relationships that would most benefit them. Therefore, they end up with unbalanced, lopsided lives. Once you understand the 80/20 principle, please ask yourself this critical question: *why should I settle for an unbalanced life when there is a clear alternative, namely, determining which kinds of actions generate most of my desired results and then engaging more and more in those kinds of actions rather than any alternatives?* It's a question worth asking repeatedly.

For example, assuming that you have read # 24 and don't yet have your conversion book done, have you taken action to get your conversion book started or are you content merely to keep reading?

For example, are you using video to generate more leads? If not, you should be. This leads to the next suggestion.

27. Failing to Use Online Video

If you understand #17, you understand the importance of video for marketers.

Assuming that you yourself don't know how to make videos or aren't good at making them, find an expert to help you who is. There's no mystery about doing it. It's easy to find relevant and helpful books, courses, and video-makers. Take advantage of them. By doing so, your marketing will automatically be positively differentiated from the efforts of your competitors who fail to use video.

What kind of videos should you use? I answer in #32.

What medium should you use to get your videos in front of prospects? Use as many media alternatives as possible. Don't rule out local television ads. Especially during off-peak hours, they may be less expensive than you may imagine.

Still, the best place is to use videos online. Minimally, it's the best place to start using video.

A chief reason for that is that it's very inexpensive. With minimal equipment (such as an iPad or a smart phone, which you may already own), it doesn't cost a penny to create videos and upload them to YouTube. It doesn't cost a penny to set up a YouTube channel for your business. It doesn't cost a penny to set up an effective playlist or do a Hangout [cf. #39].

It's critically important to select the appropriate keywords. It can be done manually or using software. Even without software, it need not take more than 15 minutes to do a job that's good enough. If you don't know how to select appropriate keywords, either learn how to do it yourself (and there's lots of software available to make it less tedious) or find someone who does know how to help you. If you do the research yourself, it'll be time well spent. If you have to pay someone to do it for you, it shouldn't cost very much money at all because it won't take anyone who understands how to do it that long, especially if that person uses good software.

Now, once you have appropriate keywords, understand that, as an expert in your field, you already have plenty of content for doing videos. If you have gotten your conversion book done, you already have that content ready to go.

What is that content? That content is the answers to objections or confusions that prospects already have. Again, I assume that your product or service, your offering, would sufficiently help those people who are in the market for it; I assume that it will benefit them more than it costs them to purchase it. In other words, your offering has good value to your prospects.

Why, then, don't all prospects buy it? There are several reasons.

First, they may not know about it. Videos can help solve that problem.

Second, they may think that it's too expensive. Videos can help you to teach them why it's actually free, in other words, why purchasing it will give them more value than its price. Use videos to help them to understand the difference between initial price and long-term cost.

Third, they are blocked by objections, misunderstandings, or confusion. Use videos to alleviate those conditions.

In other words, since you deal with them every business day, you already understand the common objections that potential purchasers have. If you could sit down with each prospect and personally explain the answers to those objections, you'd sell more, wouldn't you? It's impossible to do that with every potential prospect, but with "taking head" videos you are able to do the next best thing, namely, personally explaining in the video to each viewer what that viewer should understand. Furthermore, those explanations are available to prospects for free 24 hours a day.

You have the answers to common objections that could benefit your prospects. Use videos to disseminate those answers.

How? That questions leads to the next topic.

28. Failing to Produce Enough Videos

If you are serious about growing your business, as soon as you understand the content of #26, you'll naturally begin to identify those specific products or services that have the most value and begin to think about promoting them more and other products or services that you offer less.

If you are serious about growing your business, as soon as you understand #17 and #27, you'll naturally begin focusing on using videos to promote your offerings.

How do I recommend that you begin as soon as possible to use videos to promote your most valuable products or services?

Video blogging.

I am not talking about making video commercials. Video blogging has nothing directly to do with selling anything.

Video blogging is about education. What's the ultimate stealthy marketing? Education.

What do prospects want to know? What should prospects know?

They should know how your "free" offering can help improve their lives.

How do you teach them that?

Show them how to solve their problems – and use videos to do that regularly. That's what video blogging is.

Suppose, for example, that you are a strength-training expert. You have books, courses, and coaching for sale. What's an effective way to attract more leads? Video blogging.

Simply set up a YouTube channel for your business and regularly upload short videos to it that strength trainees might be interested in. What might they be most interested in? Solving their problems.

Suppose that three times weekly for the next six months you upload a short video to your YouTube channel and relevant playlist that solves a specific problem with respect to strength training. In its opening, identify the problem. Then clearly and concisely demonstrate how to avoid or solve it. Then suggest that a viewer do something else, which is called a "call to action" [CTA].

Do you have the understanding to do that? As a strength training expert, yes.

Do you have the equipment necessary to do that? If you have a computer and some kind of video camera, yes.

Do you have the understanding of how, properly, to upload the video to YouTube? Quite possibly, not yet. However, you'll understand enough if you follow the suggestions in this book – and it's very easy to find instructional videos on YouTube itself on how to do that and similar tasks.

As a matter of fact, there are relatively inexpensive online courses on video blogging available by such experts as Mike Stewart and Brad Scott. Why not buy one or two and learn from teachers who have walked the walk?

Permit me to stress that I'm not talking about video sales letters or commercials. If you do video blogging, forget about everything except helping people solve their problems. Your videos need not, and should not, be long. Often they may only last from 1 to 5 minutes, and it's usually unwise to have them last longer than 7 minutes. Your videos need not be polished or professional; for example, you do not have to shoot them in a studio. Ensuring that they have excellent audio and good enough lighting will be sufficient. Your viewer is not watching your video to purchase anything. Your viewer is watching it to learn how to solve a problem.

Suppose that you are a strength training expert and that you want to do video blogging. Using a camera on a tripod or getting a friend to shoot you, simply go to your gym and show your viewer what you want him to understand.

For example, you might demonstrate the right way to warm up or stretch a muscle group. You might have six videos on six different ways to do squats. If there are three common technique mistakes on each of those six squat varieties, you might have eighteen more videos in which you demonstrate on each a common technique mistake. So there's two dozen videos just about squats – and you could easily come up with dozens of more videos on proper and improper techniques with respect to all the other different kinds of exercises such as deadlifts, presses, pull-ups or pull-downs, bicep curls, calf raises, hamstring curls, and so on and on.

But, you may object, there are already strength training experts with channels on YouTube who already do that. So? They are not you. Don't be afraid to inject a little personality or fun into your videos. Be caring, too. Really help trainees to benefit from strength training without getting injured. Enable them to begin thinking of you as their wise strength-training coach. Lead with the giving hand. Let them relate to you. Let them feel confident that you understand how to help and will never lead them astray.

Make sense?

As in anything else, initially you'll have to force yourself consistently to make those videos. It'll get easier and easier as you practice and get better at doing it. Your efficiency will improve and, soon, you'll be able to make a video for your blog in under half an hour. If you make 3 videos weekly, you'll be spending less than 90 minutes weekly positioning yourself as a friendly, helpful expert in your field. It'll be exciting to watch the number of subscribers to your channel keep increasing. In six months you'll have nearly 80 helpful videos available. Who except an expert would do that many videos on a topic?

Do you think that may eventually reward you? Doyathink? What goes around comes around. It's not only important to lead with the giving hand, it may be impossible to give more than you receive.

29. Settling for Improper Equipment

Cameras and software are so good these days that the worst mistake with respect to video equipment is no more expensive to cure than obtaining an excellent microphone.

If you already have a camcorder, an iPad, an iPhone, an Android phone, a [920 or 930] Logitech webcam, or a digital camera that takes videos, you already have a camera that will work. If you don't have a camera and need to buy one, I recommend buying an iPad – and you need not buy the latest generation.

Excellent audio is critical. I recommend some kind of USB microphone. You can purchase one relatively inexpensively; for example, a Blue Yeti is available for under $50. You may use a wired lapel microphone such as Giant Squid or Microphone Madness.

If you have a friend who is readily available regularly and willing to shoot you, you don't need a tripod. If not, you'll need a tripod. They can be expensive. Consider starting with an inexpensive one if you need one and upgrading when your income grows.

Lighting can be expensive or relatively inexpensive. It depends upon what you are able to afford. A light box kit with 2 lights for around $150 will work fine forever, but there are less expensive alternatives that will work.

It's best to have a simple, relatively uncluttered background. A large whiteboard is fine. There's no need initially to invest in anything fancy or expensive such as a green screen cloth with frame.

Editing software is important. A good, inexpensive choice is Screencast-o-matic. I use Camtasia, which is expensive but is sometimes available at a discount and is available for either PC or Mac. Many who have a Mac prefer Screenflow. If you have a PC, you'll never need more than Camtasia, but you could go up to Sony Vegas. Taking the time to edit each video properly is critical to producing high-quality videos. Spending a little time to ensure that each video you make is well (or at least decently) edited is an excellent practice. [See #33.]

Again, the main mistake here is to permit poor audio quality. The second worst mistake is not editing videos at all.

30. Not Using Others' Ideas for Content

Are you the font of all wisdom and knowledge? I didn't think so.

Ideas cannot be copyright or patented. There's nothing illegal or immoral about using ideas that you initially learned from others. If we all weren't used to doing that, we'd probably still be crawling instead of walking.

However, make an idea your own before passing it along. Be sure to test it sufficiently so that you are willing to have it identified with you. When you sign on to something, you own it. Protect your reputation.

It's always a good idea to give credit where credit is due. If you pick up an idea or technique from someone else, why not give them some credit for it? It's one thing if you are unable to remember where you learned something, but it's another thing deliberately to steal or use someone else's idea without attribution. Besides, instead of blaming you for not being original, others will think more highly of you for doing research as well as for demonstrating integrity.

I'm not sure that any of the ideas in this book on marketing or video marketing are original with me. So? Do you care? Probably not. What you probably care about is whether or not they are effective. In case you do care, in the Acknowledgements section, I tell you who my teachers have been and encourage you, too, to learn from them as well as from me.

The same is true for all my important ideas in philosophy. I am unable even to think of any major ones that I accept that were original with me. So? We all stand on the shoulders of our predecessors.

Originality is often overrated; it's also important to preserve and transmit good ideas as well as to diminish or destroy bad ideas.

Your videos will be original simply because you created them. Any ideas you learned from others will be filtered through your conceptual system. You may be unable to think of a new way to squat effectively, but how you teach proper squat technique may nevertheless be quite effective as well as original with you. Your viewers don't really care where your content came from. They want to know how, for example, to squat effectively without getting injured.

How can you get lots of good ideas to use in your videos? Get lots of ideas. Open up to ideas that are new to you.

How can you get lots of ideas? Continuing education. How many books do you read each month? How many courses do you take each year? How many conferences or conventions do you attend yearly? How often to you watch online educational videos or listen to audio programs? If you deliberately keep learning, you'll not be able to avoid encountering lots of ideas that are new to you.

As you encounter lots of ideas, some will appeal to you and some won't. Test the ones that appeal to you. Let others know the results of your tests. In other words, be intellectually alive and always open to good ideas that are new to you.

It always astounds me when I enter someone's home and don't find it overflowing with books. The value of the wisdom contained in a single $10 or $20 book may be incalculable. If you want to be a leader in business or anywhere else, you must be a reader.

Since you are already reading this book, there's no need for more preaching. Let's attend next to someone else who uses your content.

31. Failing to Brand Videos

Let's assume that you start video blogging and soon have dozens of helpful videos on your YouTube channel. Ideally, you'd like even more exposure for your videos. The good news is that YouTube makes that very easy.

As long as you permit it, anyone can "embed" one of your videos on a website by simply copying and pasting a code that YouTube automatically provides. Anyone can also copy a code that links to your YouTube video and paste that code on a website.

You want to permit others to do that. Ideally, you'd like your videos to be shared and, even, to be widely shared (to go viral).

However, there's a problem. If your video is not properly branded, that sharing won't help your business. Therefore, it's important always to brand your videos.

One way to do it is simply to watermark them with your company's logo. It's not difficult to learn how to do that with relatively inexpensive graphics software and it can be done very quickly.

Another way is to have your CTA appear in the video itself. For example, it could appear as the name of your company's website or a phone number you want someone to call. With the right video management software [such as Simple Video Pro] it's even possible to put clickable links right on the video. Such links could go to your website or a landing page.

The mistake here is not doing something to ensure that your video will be able to do what it is intended to do regardless of how many times it is shared. If you want viewers to be able to subscribe to your YouTube

103

channel, for example, then you want to ensure that they are able to do that even if they happen to watch your video on someone else's website.

32. Settling for Only One Kind of Video

In #21 I argue that it's an important mistake to fail to adjust your teaching so that it's appealing to more than one kind of learner. The chief point here is that it's also an important mistake to fail to use different kinds of teaching videos even for one viewer. In other words, it's a good idea to appeal even to the same viewer with different kinds of videos. Such variety can be important.

What are the different kinds of videos? There are three basic types.

First, there are talking head videos. These present someone talking about something. Think, for example, of a television newscaster reading the news or a television meteorologist talking about the weather in front of a map.

Second, there are presentation videos. These present either a series of screenshots such as slides, show a process on a monitor such as how to upload a video to YouTube that are often used for teaching, or present a sequence of messages using a whiteboard.

Third, there are animated videos that are similar to cartoons.

These basic types can be blended with editing software. For example, instead of simply talking a viewer through a series of slides when you are not visible, it's not difficult to use editing software to have a video of you in, say, the lower right corner of each slide that is taken by a webcam showing you talking as you go through the slides. This can be an effective blend of a slideshow presentation with a talking head video because it's more personalized than merely seeing a set of slides and listening to someone talk about them. We are, after all, social creatures who are naturally more interested in people than in slideshows or cartoons.

As you might expect, the basic types are more effective in different applications. If you are making videos and fail to understand the best uses for the different kinds of videos, your marketing will not be as effective as it should be.

In general, the most effective kind of video for getting viewers to know, like, and trust you are talking head videos. For this reason, in general most of your videos should be talking head videos.

If you lack confidence, think that your face is better suited for audio, or just are reluctant to get in front of a camera, discipline yourself to do it anyway. After all, you are the expert who is there to help prospects solve their problems. You understand that people would rather do business with other people than with companies, so make it easy for them to do business with you by getting in front of a camera. You may be able to do that in the privacy of your own home with, at most, a single friend present who is using the camera. It's not a big deal. If you are reluctant, chide yourself for being so egocentric [see #1], detach from your self-centered attachments, and do what you should do to help others more effectively.

The most important problem with respect to talking head videos is that they can be boring. There are ways to alleviate this. For example, if you shoot with two cameras, you can edit them so that the viewer goes from one angle to another when watching the finished video. If you have a friend shooting you, you can have your friend zoom in and zoom out or move the camera to different angles. Once you understand how to record them properly by, for example, using a webcam directly connected to your editing software, you'll be able to zoom in and out to create the appearance of motion during the editing process. Your videos should be as short as possible. The shorter the video, the less this is a problem.

Presentation videos don't have that problem, which is one reason why they are good for teaching. They enable teachers to show or demonstrate processes or to make a series of slides that, especially if they are attractive with easy-to-follow bullet points, are often very effective in helping a viewer understand how to solve a problem. What the viewer is seeing changes frequently. On the other hand, of course, they are impersonal in the sense that it's impossible for their viewers to identify either with a set of slides or processes that are shown on a computer monitor.

The best use for animated videos is driving online traffic. While whiteboard videos can substitute for slideshow presentations when teaching, driving traffic is the best way to use animated videos for business. Unlike talking head videos, they are impersonal. Unlike screencast videos, they are not good at teaching. They can, especially if short and well-scripted with a story, be entertaining and nonthreatening. There's terrific, relatively inexpensive software available [such as Explaindio, Video Maker FX, or Easy Sketch Pro (I own all three)] that make animated videos easy to make. However, my recommendation is that, unless you are using them to drive traffic to somewhere else, be reluctant to use them. Since driving online traffic is important, it of course does not follow that you shouldn't use animated videos.

33. Insufficient Video Editing

Is the editing more important than the raw footage? Often. So don't make the mistake of not editing your video sufficiently.

A poem that has an extra word or omits a word isn't a great poem. However, please don't think of your videos as like works of art. Given the 80/20 principle [#26], you should not even aim to make your videos great. They only have to be good enough.

However, they should be good enough. What's that? Let's first review some characteristics they should have that I mention elsewhere in this book:

They should be as short as possible to cover what you need to say. 7 minutes is a good maximum length. About 4 minutes would be better. Especially if you are only driving traffic, you may find that the sweet spot is from about 45 seconds to 2 minutes.

They should have excellent sound quality. Sound levels should be good. Any background music should be neither too loud nor too soft. Always use an excellent microphone.

They should have good lighting and video quality.

Their content should help someone solve a problem.

It's best if they are "edutainment," in other words neither all education nor all entertainment. Let the best aspects of your personality shine so they aren't boring.

Every video should end with a CTA: you're the expert, so tell a viewer what to do next and provide a reason for doing it.

Speak your viewer's language. If you must use technical terms, when you introduce them always define them using nontechnical language. If possible, use simple language that any bright 12-year-old is able to understand.

Do sprinkle in keywords lightly. If you post a video on YouTube, there will be an automatic transcript made of it and those keywords will be helpful for SEO. On the other hand, don't stuff it with keywords.

Let's next consider some characteristics that I don't mention elsewhere in this book:

Speak about 20% louder on videos than you usually do and speak at least 20% faster than you usually do when you are recording a video. This will reduce viewer boredom and communicate enthusiasm.

Although it depends upon the distance between the camera and you, it's usually best to make your gestures "bigger" than they'd normally be. The reason for this is that a camera tends to deaden movement. The exception to this occurs if you are really close to the camera; in that case, make your gestures "smaller" than they'd normally be.

It's important to have music in their backgrounds. Ensure that it is royalty-free music, in other words, that you have the legal right to use it. Notice that movies, television shows, and commercials almost always without exception have music. When you use music, your video instantly seems more professional. It creates a more powerful emotional impact. It alerts viewers to pay attention: when they hear music, they know the show has begun. It differentiates your videos from all those other video makers who don't use music. It's easy to add during the editing process, and it need not be expensive. Take 2 or 3 seconds to fade it in in the beginning of your videos and 2 or 3 seconds to fade it out at their ends. It need not be at all expensive to build up a music library of background sound tracks.

Make use of lower-thirds. It's not difficult to add words onto your videos during the editing process. Add them to the lower third of what a viewer sees when watching a talking head video. Ensure, of course, that there is good contrast between the color of their text and the background color of the lower third so that they are easily legible. You may add in names, URL's to websites or YouTube or other places like Vimeo where there is a relevant video, phone numbers, or relevant CTA's. You may want to add in bullet points to emphasize the chief points that you are speaking about in the video.

Remember: you are shooting your own videos and they are short. Since everything is already set up, it hardly takes much extra time to re-shoot a video. Why not shoot a video several times? That practicing will almost always result in a superior video. If you are going to make one anyway, why not make one that is well-rehearsed as well as well edited? You won't only be more proud of it, but it's likely to be more effective.

34. Not Enabling Videos to Load Fast

For short videos such as the kind I recommend in this book, load speed is not normally an important issue. Still, I recommend that you avoid the mistake of not enabling your videos to load as quickly as possible.

How?

Use Handbrake. It's free software that you should run every video through before you upload it anywhere.

To enable it, go to handbrake.com and download it to your computer.

To use it, open it by clicking on its icon. Click on "Source" in the upper left, find the video you want on your computer, and load it into Handbrake. In "Output setting," check "Web Optimized." You may leave all the other settings on default or change them as you desire. Then select "Start" in the upper left. That's it!

You have optimized your video to load as quickly as possible. Then upload your video to YouTube or wherever you want to use it.

35. Not Optimizing Your Channel or Videos

It's important to optimize your YouTube channel as well as each of your videos.

Here's how to set-up your YouTube channel properly:

Login to your Google account. (They are free, so, if you don't have one, open one.) Using the dropdown menu in the upper right, go to YouTube to switch accounts. Select "all my channels" and then "create a new channel" when it opens. There's no need to verify a channel for your business video blog (unless you are going to have videos longer than 15 minutes, which I don't recommend).

There's no one best way to name your channel. Google seems to like it if you personalize it by using your own name. You may use the name of your product or service. It may be best, though, to use your best keyword as the name of your YouTube channel. Don't put personal or extraneous videos on the same channel as your business video blog; that would just create confusion.

You will need to add channel art. If you have some graphics software and understand how to use it, it should be 2560 x 1440 pixels (with a 2 MB max). If you don't, simply go to somewhere like fiverr.com and have someone inexpensively make you something suitable.

It's a good idea to use either a headshot photo of you or company logo for your Gmail account. It will automatically appear in a little box in your channel art.

In settings, edit your channel's description. What's your channel about? Take a little time with your description because it's relevant for search engine optimization (SEO). Be thorough and sprinkle relevant keywords throughout your description. It'd be best to do a little research, even just on YouTube itself, for pointers on how to set up and describe your channel. Take your time and do it well. You only have to do it once.

Use "add custom link" and check "overlay link on channel art" to have a clickable link on your top banner that goes, for example, to your website's homepage or landing page.

Use "add social links" to have links to social media accounts such as Google+, LinkedIn, and so on. Use their full URL's (with, for example, the 'http://www' if appropriate) to ensure that they are clickable.

Feature any other channels you have. It's your choice whether or not to show your own subscriptions. Click 'done' to save your set up.

Here's how to optimize each of your videos initially:

It's very important to use the best keyword for the title of a video. It should be relevant to both the content of the video and its description.

I always optimize videos before uploading them to YouTube or other video sites. Here's how: find the video on your computer and right click on it. Click on 'Properties.' Click on the Details tab. Use the primary keyword as its title and the best other keyword as its sub-title. Give it a high rating. For both the tags and comments sections, enter the best 5 or 10 or 15 keyword variations. Select 'O.K.' and then upload your video.

It's important to optimize your video's description, and it's very important to optimize the first two lines of that description. Start the description with the best keyword and follow that with the full URL of the video. (Whenever you upload a video, YouTube will provide you with its URL even while it's uploading. Simply copy and paste the whole URL into the description near its beginning and again at its end.) You may follow the opening URL immediately with a CTA. Writing out a description of up to 500 words is fine, but a briefer description will do. The description should contain an occasional keyword, but don't stuff it with keywords. Ensure that the description is spaced properly so it's easy to read. I always list the keyword variations after the description. Add the full URL of the video again as the last line of the description.

Having at least one tag that is appropriate for the video is important. Again, use keywords and understand that it considers singular and plural keywords as different. 5 or 10 tags are sufficient.

Ensure that your privacy setting is "public" so that others are enable to see your video. The category you select may be appropriate, but it never seems to hurt to use "People & Blogs."

The custom thumbnail is a perk that you should use once you are permitted to do so.

Encourage likes, comments, questions, and sharing. It's your choice whether or not you want to screen them; screening them in advance is a little extra work, but it's probably worth it to weed out idiotic comments. Always respond helpfully and courteously to serious comments and questions.

It's a good idea to edit or replace your video's transcript. If you take the trouble to do it, it will help with SEO.

Once you have done it a few times, optimizing each video that you upload to YouTube doesn't take but 2 or 3 minutes.

What about off-page optimization for YouTube videos? It's possible to hire people or use software to do it effectively. As happened with respect to websites, though, that is likely to change in the future.

36. Permitting Poor Video Scripts

The most important element of a video is its script. If you closed your eyes and simply listened to it, it should still be persuasive. So it's a mistake to permit any of your videos to have poor scripts.

This does not entail that you need to write out the script for a video word-for-word in advance. In fact, unless you are a trained actor, practice reading a script several times. When we read a script, most of us don't sound at all natural. Make it as easy as possible for a viewer to relate to you. If you sound strange for whatever reason, if you don't talk like normal humans talk, you'll only succeed in making it more difficult for a normal person to relate to you. If you are using a script, the best software I've found is Content Samurai.

Similarly, the words you use should be normal words that come to mind naturally.

On the other hand, it's also a mistake just to wing it and say whatever comes to mind.

The solution is the middle way between those two extremes: talk from an outline. How?

One solution is to chunk down your material into no more than 7 bite-sized chunks of information. If you were writing out the script, each of the seven chunks would be the topic sentence of a paragraph. Since you are not writing it out, make it easy to remember those 7 or fewer points in sequence. A standard way that many speakers use is to associate each point with a room of a well-known or easily imagined house. Imagine entering and walking it. The first point is the entranceway. The second point is the living room. The third point is the kitchen. And so on. Just move naturally from point to point until your imaginary house tour is over.

Another solution is to write a list of those 7 or fewer points and put it just under the camera. If you don't keep eye contact with the camera as you are speaking, if you keep looking elsewhere, you'll come across to a viewer as shifty or dishonest. So it's important to appear to be looking at the camera. However, if you look just under the camera, a viewer will almost certainly think that you are looking directly at the camera.

Some people don't like looking at a camera lens. If you are like that, Peter Wray suggests attaching a piece of colored tape just above the lens and looking at that – or set a small teddy bear on top of it and talk to it.

It's not necessary to buy tele-prompter software, which is usually too difficult to use by yourself anyway.

Suppose that you are doing a talking head video. Since we are more energetic when standing than we are when sitting, you'll probably want to be standing up while you look at the camera while speaking. You may mount a whiteboard on a tripod or a large piece of paper just under the camera so that the points you'll need are easily read.

Another alternative for a talking head video is to have a white board behind you that lists each of your points. Have them covered up. You might, for example, cover each one with a piece of paper held by a single small piece of tape. When you want to make the next point, turn around, uncover the point by removing the paper so that the viewer can see it and you'll be reminded what it is, and then turn back to the camera and talk about it.

If you are using your webcam at your computer, it's possible to use a small piece of paper just under the webcam that lists your points. It's even possible to have your points scroll down on the computer's monitor so that you may refer to them if you hold the mouse down below a viewer's line of site and use your thumb for scrolling as quickly or slowly as necessary. Unlike tele-prompter software, this method costs nothing and it's easily possible to do it by yourself.

37. Permitting Poor Video Structure

Like other temporal productions, a video should have a beginning, middle, and end. Let's consider these in reverse order. This is an example of the fruitful tactic of beginning with the end in mind.

The end is simple: it's the CTA or close. Don't leave a viewer confused about what to do next. Explain exactly what should be done next and briefly why that's the best course of action.

The middle should present the solution to the viewer's problem. In effect, this is usually the argument for the CTA; it provides the premises for which the CTA is the conclusion. Explain clearly and simply how the problem can be alleviated or solved. Don't forget to justify the solution. You may rule out other alternatives that don't work or don't work as well. What's important is fulfilling the implicit promise in the introduction, primary key word, or title. What steps did you follow to solve the problem? Tell the story. What happened? Do you have any evidence that it may work for someone else?

The beginning offers choices. Different video marketing experts have different styles for opening a video. One feature is critical: you have at least 3 seconds and at most 11 seconds to grab a potential viewer's interest. That means that it's critical to open in such way that the viewer is enticed to keep watching.

When reading a web page, the only purpose of the headline is to stimulate the reader to read the next sentence. When beginning a video, the only purpose of the opening is to stimulate the viewer to keep watching.

Sometimes this is called a "hook" or "pattern interrupt." The idea is to intrigue the viewer. Since the only viewers you care about are the viewers who have the problem you are solving in the video, expose the problem. Forget about viewers who don't have that problem. It's often a good idea to agitate it, to draw out its disastrous implications if left unsolved. If you are able to relate it to a storyline [mentioned in # 13], excellent.

Be on the alert for scams relating to your niche. Why? Explaining to a viewer how to avoid being taken advantage of is an evergreen tactic that will earn you good will. You'll be perceived as an expert in your niche, as an insider who both understands what's going on and is helpful to underdogs.

Test various kinds of openings until you find some that work well for you.

For example, you might open with something like: "In this 2 minute video I'll explain how I lost my job and my house and then, in one month with little effort, stumbled upon a making money online secret that made me a millionaire in three weeks." The story promised here, of course, stretches credulity, but something like that can work well as a hook.

Make your story appealing and at least somewhat credible: "In the next 3 minutes I'll tell you the story of how I lost 28 pounds in 28 days without hunger and without exercise." Wouldn't you like to hear that story?

Focus on a pain point and use words that are laden with emotion. "You know how it's so *frustrating* to want to lose weight and yet all the conflicting dietary advice is so *confusing*? I finally solved that problem when I . . ." (A very helpful book on this topic is Richard Bayan's Words that Sell.)

Agitate the problem briefly in the introduction: "My doctor told me I'd be dead in 3 months if I didn't lose some serious weight."

Understand that a viewer will be skeptical about your solution. Explain what makes you the expert. Why are you qualified to present a solution?

Why does the solution work? Give a reason. Offer proof.

With respect to the <u>end</u> of a video, the most common structural mistake is not ending with a clear CTA. Normally, the CTA will offer a shortcut to solving the problem or offer something additional with respect to the solution.

With respect to the structural <u>middle</u> of a video, if it doesn't help someone solve a problem, what good is it? If you sell good news, if you promote useful solutions, viewers will soon look forward to new videos from you. The more they enjoy and benefit from your videos, the more they will be inclined to do business with you.

With respect to the <u>beginning</u> of a video, it's critical to have a fast opening that grabs a potential viewer's attention.

If you avoid just these three basic mistakes, your videos will be much more effective than otherwise.

Incidentally, there are video marketers [for example, Peter Beattie] who offer fill-in-the-blank video scripts for various situations that you may find useful until you develop your own set of templates.

A marketing video should be only as long as it needs to be. To keep it as short as possible, keep it focused. How? Present one problem, one solution, and one CTA. Keep it simple; don't try to discuss multiple problems or multiple solutions or have multiple CTA's in one video.

38. Ignoring the Whole SERP

There's only so much space available on a SERP [search engine results page]. Think about, say, a Google SERP. There are often paid advertisements on the right side and horizontally across the page near its top. Much of the page is taken up with organic (free) rankings. Especially if most or all of the web properties that are ranked on a SERP are websites rather than videos, if you have a listing for a video, it will stand out immediately because it has a thumbnail. That may mean that it'll get clicks even if it's not among the top three.

So far, so good. There's an inherent problem though: those thumbnails take up space. If Google or some other search engine gives your thumbnail the space, that's fine. However, sometimes space is at such a premium on SERP's that no videos are listed.

Furthermore, over 60% of searches are done today from mobile devices. Obviously, what can be shown on the screen of, say, a cell phone is a lot less than what can be shown on the monitor of a desktop. This didn't used to be a problem for video marketers, but now it often is.

In fact, the initial screen that comes up on some mobile devices may not have any organic listings at all. Instead, what may initially appear is a "7 pack" of local places, which are maps. So, if your business offering doesn't show up there, then you may not receive any traffic from that page. If, therefore, you have a local store or office, it's important to get your business establishment listed in the top 7 local places. If it's not, you may be at least initially invisible to some searchers even if you have a terrific, optimized, and highly ranked website.

Furthermore, with respect to many local searches, Google is phasing in a "carousel." That's a horizontal row across the top of a SERP of thumbnails to local businesses. Again, if there's an important keyword related to your business that has a carousel and your thumbnail does not show up in that carousel, you also may be at least initially invisible to some searchers even if you have a wonderful website.

So, check. Is there a 7 pack? Is there a carousel? If so, ensure that your business shows up there. At the moment, if you understand what you are doing it's not usually particularly difficult to ensure such visibility for local buyer's keywords, but that will change sooner or later.

Furthermore, and this is the larger point, "real estate" on a SERP is not only limited but in flux. Keep abreast of the latest changes to ensure that searchers are able to find your business offerings.

Marketing videos are often more important than websites; in fact, your business may not even need a website. However, even if that's the case, you still need to be well-located on relevant SERP's. Marketing videos are a great way to do that, but they are not the only way. This leads to another important mistake.

39. Ignoring Playlists & Hangouts

It's a mistake to ignore either playlists or Google Hangouts. Both are underutilized sources of additional profit.

It may be that <u>playlists</u> are overlooked and underutilized because marketers don't realize that they are ranked separately from videos. Therefore, by simply putting your marketing videos into playlists, you enhance the chances they'll be ranked highly.

Furthermore, it's not difficult to use your playlists to make money by using videos made by others.

Each playlist should have a theme. What should the themes be for marketing videos? How to solve problems your prospects have. Each theme is, then, a category for videos.

It's not difficult to set up a new playlist. Go into your YouTube account and then into the "video manager." Click on "playlists" and then add a new playlist. (Again, there are easy-to-find video tutorials on such technical procedures. Because the procedures are subject to change, if you have any difficulty, just find a recent tutorial video to show you exactly how, for example, to add a new playlist.)

As with videos, both the titles of playlists and their descriptions are important. What category would you like to rank for? Choose that as the title of your new playlist. YouTube allows you a description of up to 500 words. Of course, set your playlist so that the public may view it. As with videos, you may allow comments and embed playlists on a website.

Once you have set up a new playlist, it's time to populate it with helpful, relevant videos. Keep Chris in mind! [Cf. # 11.] Do a YouTube search and find other people's videos that will help Chris solve problems. Add those videos to your playlist. You should next also add a note to each of the videos (because associating text with a video has at least a little impact on the ranking of that video) and it's best also to add a brief video of yours introducing each video that you use from someone else. Contextualize it briefly for Chris.

Importantly, end the series of videos with your own video and use its CTA to direct visitors to perform some desired action such as going to your landing page for a free gift or visiting your website.

That explains how you are able to profit from playlists and from videos made by others.

You may also able to profit from Google Hangouts, which are live, streaming videos. They automatically become YouTube videos. (Google owns YouTube.) If you keep them engaging and informative and optimize them properly, they can be a very important weapon in your business's marketing arsenal.

Because they are more complicated to do than videos, even though many of the mistakes in this book also apply to doing Hangouts, it's beyond the scope of this book to provide instructions on how to do a Hangout. However, the good news is that there are plenty of helpful instructional videos readily available. Not only are there YouTube videos that will walk you through the process, there are also easily available software and courses that make doing a Hangout nearly as easy as making a video. Do an unadvertised one by yourself once or twice, and you'll be ready to do a marketing Hangout.

The interview format works very well on Hangouts. Suppose, for example, that you have a product or service you'd like to pitch. Think of the 5 or 10 most important obstructions that Chris has when it comes to purchasing your offering. Simply write them down as questions. If you have a webcam, have a friend ask you those questions and answer them live. (It surely does help to practice stating your answers before the Hangouts.) Be sure to end with a CTA. Optimize the Hangout settings immediately after you finish it and you're done.

If you have a client or a friend who has something to pitch, simply do a similar kind of interview. It really helps the rankings if you are able to invite a few friends or interested parties to view your Hangout live.

Please don't make the mistake of failing to use Hangouts because you think they are too complicated. Get some help. Learn how to do them, or have someone who knows how to do them properly simply interview you. If you don't ever use Hangouts, you simply won't be marketing your offering as effectively as it could be marketed.

40: Failing to Express Gratitude

It's normal to be dissatisfied; it's not easy to live well.

However, it's possible, whatever your circumstances, to be happy right here, right now. Although we have to claim it by realizing that nothing is missing, happiness is our birthright.

There's no such thing as a happy, ungrateful person. Zig Ziglar: "Show me one happy, ungrateful person!"

If you are not mired in ignorance and self-absorption, clients are more likely to want to do business with you. Do you like to work with unhappy, ungrateful people? Others are the same way.

Even if only for marketing purposes, adopt an attitude of gratitude. It makes no difference whether you happen to *feel* grateful or not. Resolve to behave around others as if you were grateful. (Careful! If you are not grateful yet practice acting gratefully, you may actually begin to feel grateful.)

A good test of whether or not you are successfully adopting an attitude of gratitude is how you deal with obstacles. Why not think of them as like distasteful but effective medicine? You may not want the medicine, but it will cure what ails you. Learning how to overcome obstacles is the only route to success. In that sense, however much you don't want them, they are actually beneficial.

Ultimately, the attitude of gratitude comes from realizing nonseparation. Such realization can be endlessly deepened and expanded and it always results in feeling perpetually blessed. [I have written about this elsewhere, for example, in <u>Mastery in 7 Steps</u>.]

The practical takeaway? Express gratitude daily. Don't be surprised if more people become attracted to you and want more of you. If nothing else, it'll be good for business.

My grandfather had the practice of writing a letter each Thanksgiving to five people who had helped him in life, and my father often did the same thing. Do I have to add that they were both well-respected men?

Your Next Steps

What should your next steps be?

I don't know. Neither could anyone else who is unfamiliar with your specific situation.

However, why not start with video blogging and avoid the 40 mistakes covered in this book? You probably have the equipment required already on hand, and it doesn't cost a penny to begin. Set a schedule such as doing 1 or 3 weekly and force yourself to stick to it until it becomes habitual, easier, and more fun.

If you don't yet have a conversion book, I strongly recommend that you do it in order to maximize your influence on prospects in order to help them and to increase your conversion rate. Once it's done, literally hand out your book to all serious prospects instead of handing out your business card. Since education is the best stealthy marketing, your book will instantly position you as the friendly, helpful expert in your field. (I detail how to get your conversion book done in my How to Become Happily Published, which is available from amazon.com as an inexpensive paperback or for just $2.99 as an e-book.)

Publicity is better than advertising for building your business. If you are not using it, I recommend that you begin. (You may find my 12 Publicity Mistakes That Keep Marketers Poor very helpful. It's also available from amazon.com as an inexpensive paperback or for just $2.99 as an e-book.)

Thank you for purchasing and reading this book. May you become as successful as you'd like to be.

Permit me to ask a **favor**: Will you please go to amazon.com and review this book? It may help others as well as me.

Dennis E. Bradford

Dennis E. Bradford

25 July 2016
Conesus, New York

About the Author

If you are interested in an autobiographical sketch, there's one on my Author Central page: http://www.amazon.com/-/e/B0047EI11A and another one at my http://consultingphilosopher.com website.

I encourage you to connect with me on LinkedIn where there's also more information about me: http://www.linkedin.com/pub/dennis-e-bradford/1a/a2a/524/

You'll also find there how easy it is to contact me should you wish to do so.

If you are interested in finding out more about getting my help getting your book done after reading my How to Become Happily Published, go to: http://ironoxworks.com/

If you are interested in finding out more about my national media citation service, go to: http://ironoxworks.com/media-authority-publicity-icons/

If you'd like more of my writings, most of my books are available under my name at http://www.amazon.com. Simply select 'Books' and do a search for 'Dennis E Bradford'.

If you are interested in one-on-one consulting, go to http://consultingphilosopher.com/ There valuable free information about consulting there.

If you'd like more ideas about living better, I encourage you to visit my blog on wisdom and well-being: http://dennis-bradford.com . Its posts are grouped in terms of six kinds of well-being (in no particular order) on the sidebar, namely, financial, moral (inter-personal), intellectual, physical, emotional, and spiritual. I encourage you to begin with whatever interests you most. There's an enormous amount of free, valuable content there. In fact, recommending that you visit it regularly may be the most important suggestion in this book.

Peace.